Charles H. (Charles Holland) Hoole

The Apostolic Fathers

The Epistles of S. Clement, S. Ignatius, S. Barnabas, S. Polycarp

Charles H. (Charles Holland) Hoole

The Apostolic Fathers
The Epistles of S. Clement, S. Ignatius, S. Barnabas, S. Polycarp

ISBN/EAN: 9783337058197

Printed in Europe, USA, Canada, Australia, Japan

Cover: Foto ©ninafisch / pixelio.de

More available books at **www.hansebooks.com**

The Apostolic Fathers

THE EPISTLES OF

S. CLEMENT, S. IGNATIUS, S. BARNABAS,
S. POLYCARP,

TOGETHER WITH

THE MARTYRDOM OF S. IGNATIUS AND
S. POLYCARP

TRANSLATED INTO ENGLISH, WITH AN
INTRODUCTORY NOTICE

BY

CHARLES H. HOOLE, M.A.

SENIOR STUDENT OF CHRIST CHURCH, OXFORD

RIVINGTONS
London, Oxford, and Cambridge
1872

INTRODUCTION.

HE term Apostolic Fathers would mean, in its proper sense, the disciples of the Apostles of our Lord who succeeded them in the government of the Christian Church. It is, however, usually applied only to those who have left, or are supposed to have left, works behind them. These, according to the generally received account, are S. Clement of Rome, S. Barnabas, who was the disciple of S. Paul, S. Ignatius, bishop of Antioch, S. Polycarp, bishop of Smyrna, and Papias, bishop of Hierapolis; to these, at an earlier period, would have been added Dionysius the Areopagite, but the works that bear his name are now generally acknowledged to be spurious. Had even the writings of the first mentioned come down to us in a trustworthy state, we should have possessed a considerable body of literature illustrating the most interesting period of Church history. Unfortunately, this is not the case. Instead of a complete series of contemporary accounts, like the Gospels, Acts, and Epistles, which narrate the foundation of Christianity, and the theological works which are so plentiful at a later period, the age immediately succeeding that of the Apostles is illustrated only by a series of fragments, highly interesting, but,

unfortunately, of doubtful origin. The writings ascribed to the Dionysius mentioned in Acts xvii. 34, have long been known to be spurious, and were apparently composed in Egypt towards the end of the fifth century. The Shepherd of Hermas, though a work of undoubted antiquity, and scarcely later than A.D. 120, was not, in all probability, composed by the Hermas mentioned in the Epistle to the Romans. The epistle of S. Barnabas, though regarded by Clement of Alexandria, Origen, and Jerome as genuine, is not generally received by modern critics as the work of the companion of S. Paul. Papias only survives in a few fragments. The name of S. Clement has been attached to a complete body of ecclesiastical literature, composed at different periods from the first to the ninth century. But, with the exception of the first epistle to the Corinthians, none of them date from his period; and even in the first epistle, which has the best claim to be considered his work, his name is not mentioned, and its authorship is distinctly ascribed to the Church, not to the man. Finally, the works of Ignatius, though of undoubted antiquity, have come down to us in a form which makes it extremely difficult to distinguish what is genuine from what is interpolated. Still, with all these drawbacks, the quotations and notices to be found in Origen, Clement of Alexandria, and Eusebius enable us to see that we have still in our hands a body of literature which was, in the third and fourth centuries, regarded as a legacy from the age immediately succeeding that of the Apostles ; and though questions may be raised as to whether certain works came from the pen of S. Clement or S. Barnabas, there can be no doubt that they belong either to their period, or to one but little later; and, with the exception, unfortunately, of Ignatius, have come down to us much in the same form as they had in the days of Clement of Alexandria or Eusebius. They are thus the writings of men who had either conversed with the Apostles, or had at any rate lived while the Apostolic traditions were still fresh, and personal recollections of our Lord himself were hardly extinct. They are free, too, from the controversial element, which renders the works of a later period less agreeable. They may, in fact, be regarded as forming an appendix to the canonical books of the New Testament, and it is to be regretted they have attracted so little attention outside the circle of theological scholars. With these they have always been a favourite subject. Numerous editions of them have appeared during the last two centuries, and a great mass of critical material has been collected, which is still being augmented.

Into the theological aspect of these writings it does not form part of the plan of the present work to enter. But it may be remarked that the view of our religion which they present is, on the whole, the same as that given in the New Testament ;[1] and

[1] The Epistle attributed to S. Barnabas is, to some extent, an exception.

that there is no trace of such doctrines as the supremacy[1] of the Bishop of Rome, or the worship of the Blessed Virgin. On the other hand, the episcopal form of Church government was evidently firmly established, and the clergy and laity regarded as distinct. Upon the details of Church government, and the method of conducting divine service, they unfortunately throw but little light. The writings of the Apostolic Fathers were not composed with any historical purpose, and it is only indirectly, and almost as it were by accident, that they occasionally inform us of what was passing at the time. It is impossible to avoid regretting this. At the time when the Clementine epistles and the writings of Ignatius were composed, the position held by S. Peter, with regard to the foundation of the Roman Church, must have been a matter of common knowledge. The date and manner of the death of S. Paul, and the extent of his later travels, were evidently well known. The original manuscripts of the New Testament were, in all probability, in existence. Many questions which at a later

---

[1] There is certainly a tone of authority in the way in which the Church of Rome addresses the Church of Corinth, and the concluding chapter would lead us to infer that the Roman Church already exercised a certain superintendence over the European Church; but it is the Church, not the bishop who exercises this authority. It is most probable that the disputes at Corinth had been referred to the Church of Rome for solution, as the epistle opens with an apology for delay in dealing with the subject.

period learned men, like Origen and Eusebius, vainly endeavoured to settle satisfactorily, might have been then settled beyond a doubt by contemporary authority. This, however, was not to be. Neither Polycarp nor Ignatius, nor the author of the epistle to the Corinthians, had any intention of writing the history of their own time; their object was a personal one— the benefit of the individual or Churches to whom the epistles were addressed. The reader will not fail to notice the absence of any claim to inspiration or divine authority in these writings, the earlier of which are removed but so little in date from the Book of Revelations, which plainly claims divine authority. The inferiority of style, considered merely as literary compositions, will readily be seen by any one who will compare the Epistles of S. Paul to the Corinthians with those of S. Clement. The epistles of Ignatius have, at times, a fervour which reminds us of the times of the Apostles.

The object of the present edition is to put English readers in possession of such information on the subject as is necessary for understanding the general character of the literature of the Apostolic period, and to supply a translation as literal as a regard to the convenience of English readers will allow. With regard to the translations that have already appeared of these works, that of Archbishop Wake, revised by Chevallier, has always been deservedly commended. It was, however, composed at a period when the critical knowledge of the works was imperfect, and when only Latin versions of some of the books were in the hands of scholars, the Greek text of Hermas and S. Barnabas having been recovered only during the present century. The editors of the Ante-Nicene Christian Library, which also contains translations of these works, did not make it a part of their plan to supply any detailed information as to the authorship and history of the works they translated. The present translation has been made from the text of Bishop Jacobson, with the exception of the epistle of S. Barnabas, which that edition does not contain, and which has been translated from the text of Hilgenfeld's "Novum Testamentum extra Canonem receptum." Those who wish to refer to the original texts will find many excellent editions. Dressel, Hefele, and Hilgenfeld are the most recent German editors. Bishop Jacobson's edition, though it does not contain Hermas or Barnabas, is perhaps the most complete; and an edition of S. Clement of Rome, with English notes, was published in 1869 by Professor Lightfoot. To all of these the present editor is under obligation, though he has not always found it possible to acknowledge the extent. The representatives of Dr. Cureton have kindly allowed the insertion of his translation of the three Syriac Epistles of Ignatius.

The First Epistle of S. Clement to the Corinthians.

THE title given in ancient and modern times to this epistle seems hardly borne out by its contents. It is stated in the preface that it is an epistle from the Church of Rome to the Church of Corinth. "The Church of God which sojourneth at Rome to the Church of God that sojourneth at Corinth, to them that are called, sanctified by the will of God through our Lord Jesus Christ. Grace and peace be multiplied unto you from God Almighty through Jesus Christ." There is no mention of S. Clement in the epistle, nor of any person except the Roman Church as responsible for its authorship. Judging from the internal evidence, it is merely a message of warning and instruction from one Church to another. The question consequently arises, how came the name of Clement to be connected with the epistle? The earliest authorities ascribe the epistle to the Church of Rome, and not to S. Clement. Dionysius, Bishop of Corinth, writing to the Roman Church 165—175 A.D., mentions it as the epistle written to the Corinthian Church by the Roman Church διὰ Κλήμεντος, by the hand of Clement; much in the same way as various epistles of S. Paul are said to be written διὰ Τυχικοῦ καὶ Ὀνησίμου (Colossians) by the hand of Tychicus and Onesimus; διὰ Τυχικοῦ (Ephesians) by the hand of Tychicus. He thus alludes to it: "To-day we have kept the Lord's day as an holy day, and on it have read your epistle, which we shall always read for our instruction, as also the former letter which you wrote to us by the hand of Clement."[1] Irenæus, the next authority in point of time, does not even connect the name of Clement with the authorship, merely stating that in the time of Clement the Church of Rome sent a very powerful letter to the Corinthians.[2] Thus these very excellent authorities agree with the internal evidence to be derived from the epistle itself, that it is not a work of S. Clement, in the same sense as the Ignatian epistles are the work of S. Ignatius, but an epistle from the Church of Rome, adding, what we do not gather from the epistle itself, but what there seems no reason to doubt, that it was written during the episcopate of S. Clement. Later authorities—Clement of Alexandria, Origen, and Eusebius—ascribe it unhesitatingly to S. Clement;[3] but we have no

[1] τὴν σήμερον οὖν κυριακὴν ἁγίαν ἡμέραν διηγάγομεν, ἐν ᾗ ἀνέγνωμεν ὑμῶν τὴν ἐπιστολήν, ἣν ἕξομεν ἀεί ποτε ἀναγινώσκοντες νουθετεῖσθαι, ὡς καὶ τὴν προτέραν ἡμῖν διὰ Κλήμεντος γραφεῖσαν. Euseb. H. E. iv. 31, 13.

[2] ἐπὶ τούτου οὖν τοῦ Κλήμεντος στάσεως οὐκ ὀλίγης τοῖς ἐν Κορίνθῳ γενομένης ἀδελφοῖς, ἐπέστειλεν ἡ ἐν Ῥώμῃ ἐκκλησία ἱκανωτάτην γραφὴν τοῖς Κορινθίοις, εἰς εἰρήνην συμβιβάζουσα αὐτοὺς καὶ ἀνανεοῦσα. Iren. Adv. Hær. iii. 3, 3.

[3] Clement of Alexandria, Strom. i. 7, 38, p. 339, and

reason to suppose that they had any real authority for doing so, or did so in fact on any other grounds than that a tradition had sprung up after the time of Irenæus that S. Clement was in reality the author of the epistle. Such a tradition can have little weight compared with the evidence to be drawn from the epistle itself. It is difficult to suppose that if S. Clement were really the

in many other passages. Origen de Princ. ii. 3, 6 (Opp. i. 82), and in several other passages. Euseb. H. E. iii. 16. Cf. Hilgenfeld's "Novum Testamentum extra Canonem receptum," Prolegomena to S. Clement, p. xxii. The following are the passages from Eusebius : τούτου δὴ οὖν τοῦ Κλήμεντος ὁμολογουμένη μία ἐπιστολὴ φέρεται, μεγάλη τε καὶ θαυμασία, ἣν ὡς ἀπὸ τῆς Ῥωμαίων ἐκκλησίας τῇ Κορινθίων διετυπώσατο, στάσεως τηνικάδε κατὰ τὴν Κόρινθον γενομένης. ταύτην δὲ καὶ ἐν πλείσταις ἐκκλησίαις ἐπὶ τοῦ κοινοῦ δεδημοσιευμένην πάλαι τε καὶ καθ᾽ ἡμᾶς αὐτοὺς ἔγνωμεν, καὶ ὅτι γε κατὰ τὸν δηλούμενον τὰ τῆς Κορινθίων κεκίνητο στάσεως, ἀξιόχρεως μάρτυς ὁ Ἡγήσιππος. III. 39: ὥσπερ οὖν ἀμέλει τοῦ Ἰγνατίου ἐν αἷς κατελέξαμεν ἐπιστολαῖς, καὶ τοῦ Κλήμεντος ἐν τῇ ὁμολογουμένῃ παρὰ πᾶσιν, ἣν ἐκ προσώπου τῆς Ῥωμαίων ἐκκλησίας τῇ Κορινθίων διετυπώσατο, ἐν ᾗ τῆς πρὸς Ἑβραίους πολλὰ νοήματα παραθείς, ἤδη δὲ καὶ αὐτολεξεὶ ῥητοῖς τισὶν ἐξ αὐτῆς χρησάμενος, σαφέστατα παρίστησιν ὅτι μὴ νέον ὑπάρχει τὸ σύγγραμμα. . . . ἰστέον δ᾽ ὡς καὶ δευτέρα τις εἶναι λέγεται τοῦ Κλήμεντος ἐπιστολή. οὐ μὴν ἔθ᾽ ὁμοίως τῇ προτέρᾳ καὶ ταύτην γνώριμον ἐπιστάμεθα, ὅτι μηδὲ καὶ τοὺς ἀρχαίους αὐτῇ κεχρημένους ἴσμεν. . . . ἡ μὲν οὖν τοῦ Κλήμεντος ὁμολογουμένη γραφὴ πρόδηλος. H. E. vi. 13, 6 : κέχρηται δ᾽ ἐν αὐτοῖς (Stromatis) καὶ ταῖς ἀπὸ τῶν ἀντιλεγομένων γραφῶν μαρτυρίαις, τῆς τε λεγομένης Σολομῶντος Σοφίας, καὶ τῆς Ἰησοῦ τοῦ Σιράχ, καὶ τῆς πρὸς Ἑβραίους ἐπιστολῆς, τῆς τε Βαρνάβα καὶ Κλήμεντος καὶ Ἰούδα.

author of the epistle, he would not only have abstained from mentioning himself in any way throughout it, but would have stated in the preface that it was an epistle of the Church of Rome. With the very early authority of Irenæus in our hands, there can be no fair grounds for disputing the assertion that it was written during the episcopate of S. Clement; and an epistle from the Church of Rome would naturally be drawn up under the superintendence of the Bishop of Rome. In what way this was done we are not informed; but it seems reasonable to suppose that it would be in the first instance drawn up by a committee, consisting of the leading men of the Church, under the presidency of the bishop, and submitted for the approval of the whole body. It would then, in all probability, be copied by the bishop, and sent by him as the representative of the Roman to the Corinthian Church. In this way it would be what it professes to be—an epistle from the Church of Rome to the Church of Corinth, expressing the opinions, not of the individual, but of the Church.

About the date of the epistle there is a good deal of controversy. Few critics seem disposed to place it later than A.D. 100, the majority making the date about A.D. 95, and the persecution alluded to in the commencement of the epistle, the persecution under Domitian. There are not, however, wanting grounds for giving it a much earlier date. In chap. 41 the Temple of Jerusalem is spoken of as still standing,[1] and sacrifices are said to be offered there. Jerusalem was captured A.D. 70, so that, if the allusion is to be interpreted literally, the epistle could hardly have been written after that date. A certain Fortunatus also is mentioned in chap. lix. who is supposed to have been the same mentioned by S. Paul, 1 Cor. xvi. 17. The deaths of the Apostles S. Peter and S. Paul are mentioned,[2] but in a way that would certainly allow of their having very recently occurred. If we accept A.D. 67 as the date of the death of S. Paul, it would be possible to take A.D. 69 or 70 as the date of the epistle, and to make the persecution referred to as that under Nero; putting the episcopate of Clement as about A.D. 68, and his place in the succession between Linus and Anacletus.

This view, it will be remarked, is just tenable. On the other hand, with the exception of the passage about Jerusalem, the contents and general tone of the epistle harmonize better with a later date.[3] The place of Clement in the succession,

[1] The allusion to Jerusalem is in cap. xl.; the statement that sacrifices were then offered at the Temple is certainly most distinct. Cf. Hefele's note. Lightfoot, the most recent editor, prefers to interpret it as an allusion to the past, and not to consider it as settling the date of the epistle. Hefele takes the opposite view, and puts the epistle at 68-70. Dressel and Hilgenfeld give the later date; no modern editor appears to support Hefele. See Jacobson's "Patres Apostolici," i. xii. Gieseler, Eccles. Hist., i. iii.

[2] Cap. 5. S. Peter's name has been restored by conjecture. Cf. Lightfoot's note.

[3] Lightfoot's Introduction to S. Clement of Rome, p. 4.

being itself a matter of controversy, does not assist us in fixing the date of the epistle; it is, perhaps, better to consider the mention of the sacrifices at Jerusalem as one not to be construed literally, and to accept the close of the first century as the date of the epistle. Everything, however, in it betokens very great antiquity. None of the Apostles themselves seem to be alive, and there is no allusion to miraculous gifts as surviving in the Church, but some of the persons appointed by the Apostles to succeed them in the government of the Church are still living;[1] we are, consequently, in the generation succeeding that of the Apostolic era, between A.D. 70 and 100; and there seem no fair grounds for accepting the views of some modern critics, who, on the strength of an allusion to the apocryphal book of Judith, would place the composition of the epistle in the reign of Trajan.[2]

The epistle is frequently alluded to by ecclesiastical writers, from the time of Dionysius of Corinth, A.D. 167, to Antonius Melissa, A.D. 1140. The following passage from Eusebius may be taken as a specimen of the way in which it was regarded (H. E., iii. 15):—"In the twelfth year of the same emperor (Domitian) Clement succeeded Anacletus, who had been bishop of the Church of Rome for twelve years. Him the Apostle, in his Epistle to the Philippians, describes as his fellow-labourer,

---

[1] Cap. 44.
[2] Cap. 55. Cf. Lightfoot's note, where the question is discussed.

saying, "Together with Clement and the rest of my fellow-labourers, whose names are in the book of life." Of this Clement there is one epistle of acknowledged authenticity, great and admirable, which he composed as from the Roman church to that of the Corinthians, there being a dissension at that time at Corinth; and we know that this is publicly read in a great number of churches, both in former times and in our own days."

Clement of Alexandria is the earliest[1] known writer who quotes it as the epistle of Clement,[2] citing it as Clement in the epistle to the Corinthians. It is not quoted by name by Tertullian, nor is it mentioned in the decree of Gelasius; and, with the exception of a single passage in Eusebius, which bears the authority of Clement of Alexandria rather than his own, and in which the epistle is classed with the Wisdom of Solomon, the Epistle to the Hebrews, and the Book of Jesus the Son of Sirach, as among the disputed books of Scripture.[3] No attempt seems to have been made to include it in the canon: a remarkable fact, when we consider its acknowledged antiquity, and the person to whose pen it was ascribed. In the

[1] Allusions to the epistle have been traced in Hermas, Polycarp, and Ignatius. They contain, however, no definite reference to it, though in Hermas, Vis. ii. 4, the name Clement occurs. Cf. Hilgenfeld, Prolegom. to Clement, p. xxi.

[2] Strom. i. 7, 38, p. 339. Ὁ Κλήμης ἐν τῇ πρὸς Κορινθίους ἐπιστολῇ.

[3] Euseb. H. E. vi. 13, 6.

Latin Church it seems to have been little known except to the learned. It is quoted with approbation by S. Jerome,[1] who states that "Clement wrote to the Corinthians, in the person of the Roman Church, a very useful epistle, which is publicly read in certain places."

After A.D. 1140, the catena of evidence, which had been up to that time quite complete, ends abruptly, and the epistle apparently disappeared for about five centuries,[2] until A.D. 1628, at which date the Alexandrian manuscript was brought to England, as a present to Charles I. from Cyril Lucar, patriarch, first of Alexandria and then of Constantinople. At the end of this manuscript, which is one of the oldest existing of the Bible, and is generally assigned to the middle of the fifth century, the epistle to the Corinthians, together with a fragment commonly known as the second epistle of Clement to the Corinthians, was discovered. It is very singular that no other manuscript of later

---

[1] Jerome de Vir. Illustr. c. 15. Opp. ii. 853: "Scripsit (Clemens) ex persona Romanae ecclesiae ad ecclesiam Corinthiorum valde utilem epistolam, quae et in nonnullis locis publice legitur, quae mihi videtur characteri epistulae, quae sub Pauli nomine ad Hebraeos fertur, convenire. Sed et multis de eadem epistola non solum sensibus, sed iuxta verborum quoque ordinem abutitur. Omnino grandis in utraque similitudo est. Fertur et secunda eius nomine epistola, quae a veteribus reprobatur."

[2] The last quotations are by Nicon, 1060 A.D., and by Antonius Melissa, 1140, A.D. Cf. Hilgenfeld's Prolegomena, xxi.-xxvi., where the catena is given.

date should have preserved the epistle, which must have been constantly in the hands of ecclesiastical writers until the tenth or eleventh century. The great celebrity obtained by the spurious Clementine literature threw the early epistles completely into the shade, and it is not impossible that means may have been taken to remove from circulation a work which might have been made use of to throw a doubt on the authority of the Clementines. That this was done there is no direct evidence, but it is difficult otherwise to account for its disappearance. There is no doubt that the epistle preserved in the Alexandrian manuscript, and there called the first epistle of Clement to the Corinthians, is the one cited by Eusebius and other writers of the first twelve centuries. A few quotations, which occur in ancient writers, are wanting in the existing epistle; but a leaf of the Alexandrian manuscript, containing nearly a tenth of the epistle, is lost, and it has been suggested that these quotations may have been taken from the missing portion.[1] No Latin or Syriac version of the epistle is known to exist, nor have the discoveries of recent times included a single manuscript of the genuine Clementine epistle. The text, generally considered to be a good one, is consequently derived from the Alexandrian manuscript alone, corrected by the numerous quotations to be found in the works of the Fathers. The Editio Princeps appeared at

[1] The missing portion is after cap. 57. Cf. Lightfoot's S. Clement, where a good account of the manuscript is given.

Oxford in 1633, by Patrick Young. Since then it has been repeatedly edited; no less than fifteen editions having appeared.

The second epistle of Clement is a fragment for which, like the first, the Alexandrian manuscript is the only authority; the concluding leaves of the manuscript have been lost, so that the real length of the epistle is unknown. Though undoubtedly a work of great antiquity, dating in all probability from the second century, there seems not to be sufficient means for fixing either the authorship or the object of it. The form is rather that of a homily than of an epistle. It is first mentioned by Eusebius,[1] who expressly states that doubts existed as to its being a genuine work of S. Clement, and it is little quoted or referred to after his time. In the table of contents prefixed to the Alexandrian manuscript, it is called the second epistle of Clement, and its connection with the Corinthian Church is not improbable; but no really satisfactory account of its authorship seems to have been arrived at.[2]

There are several quotations which are apparently taken from some lost apocryphal gospel, such as the Gospel of the Egyptians, cap. iv., v., xii. Cap. xi. corresponds to cap. xxiii. in the first epistle,[3]

---

[1] H. E. iii. 31.

[2] For a summary of the numerous speculations as to its origin and object, none of which seem worthy of much attention, see Lightfoot's S. Clement of Rome, pp. 178, 179.

[3] In cap. iii. S. Luke and S. Matt. are quoted as Scripture.

and contains a long quotation from some other apocryphal work. The fragment has but little merit, though the author was apparently well acquainted both with the Old and New Testament. The scope is to enforce belief in the merit of our Lord, and to inculcate the practice of the ordinary Christian duties.

In this brief introductory account, the writer has confined himself to such information as may be drawn from the epistle itself, and the notices of it in ancient writers. Any attempt to deal with the life of S. Clement, or the literature connected with his name, leads into a region clouded with legend and abounding in controversy. The following circumstances, however, may be mentioned. A Clement was a fellow labourer of S. Paul at Philippi, and his name is mentioned in the epistle to the Philippians, iv. 3. There seems also to be no doubt that a Clement was bishop of Rome towards the end of the first century; for this we have the very early authority of Irenæus,[1] who gives the names of Linus, Anacletus, and Clement as those who succeeded S. Peter and S. Paul in the government of the Church of Rome. Irenæus does not, however, identify Clement the bishop with Clement the companion of S. Paul, though he states that the bishop had been a companion of the Apostles. The opinion of the early Church was undoubtedly that the Clement mentioned in the epistle, and the bishop of Rome, were the same;

[1] Iren. Adv. Hær. iii. 3.

and it is asserted by Origen and Eusebius.[1] There was also besides them a third Clement, Flavius Clemens, the son of the brother of Vespasian, Flavius Sabinus, who was put to death on a charge of Atheism by Domitian, a charge, we are told by Dio Cassius,[2] brought against many others who had run into Jewish opinions. There can be little doubt that by Jewish opinions Christianity is meant, and the date of the matyrdom of Flavius Clemens, about 96 A.D., would harmonize with the place in the succession of Roman bishops given to S. Clement by Irenæus.[3] Whether these three Clements were distinct persons, or whether the first and second, or second and third were identical, there seems no means of deciding. It should, however, be remarked that Flavius Clemens was consul A.D. 95, and that it is extremely unlikely that he could have united the function of Christian bishop and heathen consul at Rome ; and that Eusebius, who mentions Flavius Clemens, does not identify him with the bishop. At any rate, the name was sufficiently common to render it quite probable that the three Clements were distinct persons ; and the tendency to identify persons mentioned in the New Testament with those known to have been concerned with the early history of the Church is a sufficient reason for not considering as conclusive the tra-

---

[1] Origen in Joan. Tom. vi. 36. (Opp. iv. 153.) Euseb. II. E. iii. 15.   [2] Dio Cassius lxvii. 14.

[3] Hilgenfeld, Prolegomena, pp. xxvii., xxix. He apparently identifies S. Clement of Rome with Flavius Clemens.

ditional account that the Clement mentioned by
S. Paul and the bishop of Rome were the same.
There does not, however, seem any reason for
deciding that S. Clement of Rome was not the
Clement mentioned by S. Paul.

Of the life of S. Clement the bishop of Rome
nothing seems to be known with any certainty,
excepting what we gather from the following
passage in Irenæus[1]:—"The blessed Apostles
(S. Peter and S. Paul) having, therefore, founded
and built up the Church (of Rome), entrusted the
administration of the bishopric to Linus. Of this
Linus Paul makes mention in his epistles to
Timothy.[2] And Anacletus succeeds him. And
after him, third in succession to the Apostles,
Clement obtains the bishopric, who had also himself seen the blessed Apostles, and had conferred
with them, and had still the preaching of the Apostles sounding in his ears, and had their traditions
before his eyes; not alone, for there were still many
left of those who had been taught by the Apostles.
In the time of this Clement, no small dissension
arising among the brethren in Corinth, the Church
of Rome sent a very weighty epistle to the Corinthians, reconciling them to peace, and restoring
their faith, and declaring to them the traditions that they had recently received from the
Apostles."

The authority of Irenæus, confirmed as it is in
this case by Eusebius, may fairly be considered

---

[1] Iren. Adv. Hær. iii. 2. 3.   [2] Tim. II. iv. 21.

decisive. It is, however, necessary to mention that the majority of the Latin Christians maintained that S. Clement was the immediate successor of S. Peter, and that a number of other ecclesiastical writers, of whom S. Augustin is the most conspicuous, placed him between Linus and Anacletus, as second instead of third in the succession. The existence of these contradictory statements has given rise to a good deal of speculation among ecclesiastical writers as to the position of S. Clement and the early arrangements of the Roman Church; but, owing to the complete absence of anything like contemporary evidence on the subject, the results do not seem to pass beyond the region of ingenious conjecture.[1]

No act of the episcopate of S. Clement is recorded, nor is anything known about the method of his death, except that it seems most probable that he did not undergo martyrdom; for Irenæus, in his list of the early bishops of Rome down to Eleutherius, states that Telesphorus underwent martyrdom, but does not state it of any of the others. The legend that he was banished to the Chersonese by Trajan, and afterwards, by the command of the same emperor, fastened to an anchor, and thrown into the sea, does not seem to rest

---

[1] Hilgenfeld well remarks: "Per Clementem turbatus Romanorum episcoporum antiquissimorum ordo nobis non componendus, sed cognoscendus est."—Prolegomena ad Clem. p. xxix.

upon any historical foundation. The period of his death was most probably about A.D. 100.

A few remarks must be added on the unwelcome subject of the pseudo-Clementine literature.[1] In discussing such a subject, it should always be remembered that the mere production of a work under the name of another person does not necessarily imply dishonesty of purpose. The practice at the present day is far from uncommon, and no one attaches the slightest notion of immorality even to the most successful attempts; further, that at a time when critical knowledge was at an extremely low ebb, it was quite possible for men to be misled, and to suppose, in perfect good faith, that works had come from the hand of an early Father of the Church, which, by a modern critic, are seen at once to be spurious. How far these considerations apply to the Clementine forgeries the present writer does not presume to state. The mass of spurious literature existing under the name of S. Clement may thus be divided :—

1. Two epistles on Virginity. These exist only in Syriac; though generally acknowledged to be spurious, they are supposed to date from the middle of the second century.

2. The work called the Clementines : a collec-

---

[1] The chief authorities on the pseudo-Clementine writings are given in Lightfoot's S. Clement, p. 21. The English reader may refer to Milman's Latin Christianity, iii. 190, for an account of the False Decretals.

tion of Homilies, probably written at Rome about the latter part of the second century.[1]

3. The Clementine Recognitions; a work which is only extant in the Latin translation of Rufinus, and which is ascribed to the period between 212 and 230. It is probably of Alexandrian origin.[2]

4. The Apostolical Constitutions: a collection of rules drawn up apparently at different periods, and by different authors.

5. Various other epistles, seven of which still exist, made their appearance at different periods, three of them as late as the ninth century. The exact number does not seem to be known, but five of them are found in the False Decretals; two of these are interpolated copies of the Epistles to S. James, the brother of our Lord, both of considerable antiquity, though undoubtedly spurious; and the others forgeries by the author of the Decretals, about A.D. 829.

Of this collection, nothing can fairly claim to have come from the pen of S. Clement. The Homilies are a valuable relic of the second century, written apparently by a philosophical Christian at Rome,[3] to enforce what he considered to be the true view of religion. The Recognitions were written apparently by an Alexandrian for a similar purpose, and most probably without any dishonest intention. The Apostolical Constitutions and Canons were most probably ascribed to S. Clement as a

[1] Gieseler, i. 206.
[2] Cf. Gieseler, i. 206.   [3] Cf. Gieseler, i. 211.

kind of typical personage. They date from the third, fourth, and fifth centuries. The forged Decretals—a collection of letters and decrees of the earliest popes, and the acts of several unauthentic councils, which made their appearance in France between A.D. 829—847, and of which the five Clementine epistles are the starting-point—were undoubtedly drawn up to secure the supremacy of the Roman Church, which is, curiously enough, expressly disclaimed in the genuine Clementine epistle to the Corinthians.[1]

The object of the epistle ascribed to S. Clement was to appease certain feuds that had arisen in the Corinthian Church. The exact nature of them does not seem to be known; but they appear not to have been of a doctrinal character, but rather a struggle for pre-eminence in the Church. Even in the time of S. Paul the Corinthian Church had been open to blame for its contentious spirit and its tendency to divide into parties. "Now I beseech you, brethren, by the name of our Lord Jesus Christ, that ye all speak the same thing, and that there be no divisions among you; but that ye be perfectly joined together in the same mind and in the same judgment. For it hath been declared unto me of you, my brethren, by them which are of the house of Chloe, that there are contentions among you. Now this I say, that every one of you saith, I am of Paul, and I of Apollos, and I of Cephas, and

---

[1] S. Clement to the Corinthians, i. 7.

I of Christ." (1 Cor. i. 10–12.) There is no reference to these parties in the Clementine epistle, but rather a general reference to jealousy and envy; over-prosperity had led to luxury; the mean man had exalted himself against his superior, the foolish against the wise, the young against the old. Altogether, the picture is one of an ordinary struggle for supremacy in the Church, which had led to dissensions of a serious character, respecting which advice had been sought from the Roman Church. It came couched in very general terms, which do not let us know much of the internal state of the Corinthian Church. The epistle consists chiefly of exhortations to unity, enforced by examples from Old Testament history. In cap. v. there is an interesting allusion to the travels of S. Paul, who is said to have reached the boundary of the west, an allusion which many interpret to refer to a visit to Spain, which the Apostle had evidently once contemplated.[1] The name of S. Peter, which occurs just before, has been supplied from conjecture, the last syllable, "os," being all that is legible in the manuscript. In cap. xxiv.–xxvii. occurs an argument in favour of the resurrection, introduced apparently incidentally, but not unlikely owing to the continuance of controversies on the subject which had existed in the Church at Corinth in the time of S. Paul.[2] In the course of the argument occurs an illustration more likely than any other to offend modern tastes; the fable of the Phœnix being introduced as an

---

[1] Romans, xv. 24.   [2] 1 Cor. xv.

argument for the resurrection.[1] The belief in the existence of this bird, which is said to have arisen from mistaking an astronomical symbol for a real bird, "the appearance of the Phœnix being the recurrence of a period marked by the heliacal rising of some prominent star or constellation,"[2] was universal at the time of S. Clement. A Phœnix was exhibited at Rome A.D. 47, and it is described in works on natural history, such as Ælian. Its introduction, therefore, as an illustration, need not be regarded as detracting seriously from the value of the epistle. There is no allusion to miraculous gifts as still existing in the Church, nor do any of the Apostles seem to have been alive when the epistle was written, though some of their successors were.[3]

Only one book of the New Testament is quoted by name, the First Epistle of S. Paul to the Corinthians, cap. i. 12.[4] There are, however, allusions to several others, and many coincidences of expression with the Epistle to the Hebrews. There are two quotations of considerable length from the Gospels, in cap. xiii. and xlvi. Neither of these is exactly in the form found in any one Gospel, though the substance and the sense are the same. This is possibly merely from inaccuracy of quotation, many of the quotations from the Old Testament being equally loose. It is possible that

[1] Cap. xxv.
[2] Lightfoot, S. Clement of Rome, note to cap. xxv.
[3] Cap. xliv. [4] Cap. xlvii.

an apocryphal gospel, such as the Gospel of the Egyptains, may have been used; but this does not seem to be made out. The quotations from the Old Testament are very numerous. They are from the Septuagint version, sometimes very accurately, but often very loosely given, being most likely quoted from memory. Notice the first use of the word laity, as a distinct order;[1] the first occurrence of the word πανάγιος;[2] the first mention of the Book of Judith;[3] also the expression, God of Ages.[4]

One or two doubtful points occur in the epistle. The Danaides and Dirce, mentioned in cap. vi., cannot be identified, and the reading is possibly corrupt.[5] A saying of Moses, quoted in cap. xvii., is not found in any canonical or apocryphal work, and quotations in cap. xxiii. and xlvi. cannot be identified. They most likely come from lost apocryphal books, such as the Assumption of Moses, or the Book of Eldad and Medad. An allusion to America has been traced in the expression, "Worlds beyond the ocean."[6] The epistle shows the influence of classical authors, and especially of Sophocles,[7] though there are no direct quotations. Generally speaking, the literary character of the epistle is a little disappointing from the absence of original power and the constant tendency to reproduce the language and teaching of the Old Testament. It contains, however,

[1] Cap. xl.
[2] Cap. xxxv.
[3] Cap. lv.
[4] Ibid.
[5] Cf. Lightfoot's note.
[6] Cap. xx.
[7] Cap. xx. and xxiv.

some eloquent passages, especially cap. xx., xxiv. ; compare also xlix. with 1 Cor. xiii. One of its most pleasing features is the absence of any allusion to doctrinal controversies, and the acceptance of a common Christianity as an acknowledged ground of appeal. The Greek in which it is written is of the ordinary Hellenistic type, and does not call for much notice ; it is, however, of a purer character than the existing text of Barnabas, and less rugged than Ignatius.

A translation of several fragments has been given at the end of these two epistles ; the first two are from the Second Epistle to the Corinthians, the others seem to belong to the later Clementine writings.

The following is a short analysis of the epistle :—

The salutation of the Church of Rome to the Church of Corinth.

I. The subject of the epistle is mentioned—the seditious disturbances that had broken out in the Corinthian Church. II., III. The former happy state of the Corinthian Church is contrasted with the present disturbances ; emulation and envy, arising out of excessive prosperity, being mentioned as the cause. IV. Examples from Old Testament history of the evils caused by envy. V., VI. Examples from the present condition of the Church. VII. A practical application of the above considerations ; repentance and faith in Christ are especially enforced. VIII.—XII. Numerous examples from Old Testament history inform us of the importance of repentance and faith. XIII., XIV. Let us follow these excellent examples, being obedient to God, rather than to the leaders of sedition. XV. This is the teaching of the Old Testament, and also of our Lord Jesus Christ, of whom the prophets wrote. XVI.–XVIII. Further examples from the Old Testament. XIX.–XXI. Let us remember our proper relation to God, which the whole of his creation observes; let us beware, lest we should not be found occupying our proper position with regard to him. XXII. Quotations from the Old Testament are given to enforce this. XXIII. Let us avoid doubt and double-mindedness. XXIV. Let us especially consider the great doctrine of the Resurrection, how it is shown to us by the changes in the natural world. XXV. That marvellous bird the Phœnix is an emblem of it. XXVI. It is alluded to in the Old Testament. XXVII., XXVIII. Let us abide in this hope, and live in the fear of God. XXIX. This again is the teaching of the Old Testament. XXX.–XXXII. The following of righteousness is enforced by the example of Abraham. XXXIII. By the goodness of God manifested in creation. XXXIV. Let us imitate the harmony of the Holy Angels. XXXV. Great is the reward of righteousness; let us strive to obtain it by well doing. XXXVI. This is the way which leads us to Christ, the source of our salvation. XXXVII. We are the soldiers of Christ; let us obey our commander. XXXVIII. Let each give way to his neighbour, remembering

from whom we have received our gifts. XXXIX.
For what is the strength of man? XL., XLI. Let
us do all things decently and in order. XLII.
Bishops and Deacons were ordained by the
Apostles, in obedience to the divine command.
XLIII. Moses set the example of appeasing ecclesiastical tumults. XLIV. The Bishops appointed
by the Apostles have a claim to our obedience.
XLV. A reference to the Old Testament teaches
obedience. XLVI. Your dissensions cause harm
to many. XLVII. Ye have already been rebuked
by S. Paul for your dissensions; your present
ones are worse. XLVIII. Repent, therefore, and
return to harmony. XLIX. Great are the excel-
lences of charity. L. Let us pray that we may
attain to it. LI. Let the authors of the dissension
make confession of their guilt. LII. For such
conduct is well pleasing unto God. LIII. Moses
set an example of charity. LIV. He who hath
charity would sooner withdraw than cause dissension. LV. Many are the examples of charity.
LVI. Let us admonish each other; such admonition, as the Scripture teaches, brings us to God.
LVII. Let the authors of the seditions submit themselves to the Presbyters, so that they may escape
the punishment denounced in Scripture against the
rebellious. LVIII. May God grant to every one
who calls upon Him all righteousness. LIX. We
have sent messengers unto you, from whom we
hope to receive tidings of the restoration of peace.
Grace be with you.

The Epistle of S. Barnabas.

We owe to the discovery of the Codex Sinaiticus the Greek text of the epistle of S. Barnabas.[1] In that manuscript it comes at the end of the New Testament, between the Book of Revelation and the Shepherd of Hermas, with which the manuscript concludes. The heading is simply, the Epistle of Barnabas, and the title is repeated at the end. Previous to the discovery of this manuscript, though a considerable portion of the Greek remained, chapters i.-v. were lost, and the epistle was known chiefly by an ancient Latin version, which

[1] The plan of this work will not allow a lengthened statement of the controversy as to the authorship of the epistle of S. Barnabas. It has found its defenders in modern times, the most eminent of whom is Gieseler, whose words may be quoted: "The chief ground urged against the genuineness, that the absurd mystical mode of interpretation could not have proceeded from the companion of S. Paul, seems to me untenable. That Barnabas was not a man of spiritual consequence is clear, even from the Acts of the Apostles. There he is at first the more prominent by virtue of his apostolical commission in company with Paul. (Acts XI. 22., XII. 2.) But he soon falls entirely into the background behind Paul, after a fresh sphere of activity has commenced. (XIII. 13. 43.) Gieseler I. III., note. The modern editors, Dressel (Prolegom., p. x. xi.), Hefele (Prolegom. p. xx.), Hilgenfeld (Prolegom. p. xi.), are decided in their opposition to its genuineness, and this opinion is accepted by English scholars like Westcott and Donaldson. The strength of the external evidence in its favour is certainly considerable; and sup-

is itself imperfect, the three concluding chapters
being lost; the portion which remained in Greek
furnished only a very inferior text, and the epistle
could not consequently be read in a state which
would assure us that we had the work in the same
shape as it presented in the Ante-Nicene period.
The testimony of Hilgenfeld, who is certainly
not given to credulity in these matters, and who
personally collated the Codex Sinaiticus, is a
sufficient proof of the genuineness and importance
of the discovery; and it is from his text, as given
in the "Novum Testamentum extra Canonem receptum," that the following translation has been
made. Few, however, will agree with the sentence
with which he introduces it. "The Codex Sinaiticus
has added the Epistle of Barnabas to the Canonical
books of the New Testament."[1] No attempt seems
ever to have been made to include it in the Canon.

posing that the life of Barnabas was prolonged until after
the capture of Jerusalem—and there is no proof to the contrary—there seems nothing in the epistle that might not have
been written by him. The opposition is chiefly based on
the grounds that it is unworthy of the companion of
S. Paul, and unlike what S. Barnabas would have written.
"Totus enim tractandi modus, resque ipsæ pertractatæ,"
Dressel remarks, are the grounds for rejecting; it not generally
very safe grounds for rejecting a work, but in this case
accepted as sufficient by writers of very different views. It
should be remembered that the epistle is not quoted by
Irenæus, or by any writer earlier than Clement of Alexandria,
and that no claim seems to have been raised for its admission
into the Canon.

[1] Hilgenfeld, Prolegom. to Barnabas, p. vii.

It never seems to have risen above the level of an apocryphal book, and is mentioned as such by Eusebius and Jerome.

The following notices will show the opinion in which it was regarded in antiquity.

Clement of Alexandria.—But I need not more arguments, having as a witness the Apostle Barnabas, who was one of the seventy, and a fellow labourer of Paul, who thus speaks, "Before we believed in God, &c.," quoting from cap. xvi.[1]

Origen.—It is written in the catholic epistle of Barnabas that Jesus chose as his own disciples men who were sinful beyond all measure.[2]

Eusebius.—Among the spurious writings, let there be reckoned the acts of Paul, the book called the Shepherd, the Revelation of Peter, and, in addition to these, the reputed epistle to Barnabas.[3]

Jerome.—Barnabas the Cyprian, who is also Joseph a Levite, was ordained, together with Paul, as the apostle of the Gentiles, and composed the

[1] Strom. II. 20, 116, p. 489 : οὔ μοι δεῖ πλειόνων λόγων παραθεμένῳ μάρτυν τὸν ἀποστολικὸν Βαρνάβαν . . ὁ δὲ τῶν ἑβδομήκοντα ἦν καὶ συνεργὸς τοῦ Παύλου . . κατὰ λέξιν ὧδέ πως λέγοντα, Πρὸ τοῦ ἡμᾶς πιστεῦσαι τῷ Θεῷ, κ.τ.λ.

[2] Origenes c. Celsum I. 63 (Opp. ed. Ruae. I. 378): γέγραπται δὲ ἐν τῇ Βαρνάβα καθολικῇ ἐπιστολῇ—ὅθεν ὁ Κέλσος λαβὼν τάχα εἶναι ἐπιρρήτους καὶ πονηροτάτους τοὺς ἀποστόλους—ὅτι ἐξελέξατο τοὺς ἰδίους ἀποστόλους Ἰησοῦς ὄντας ὑπὲρ πᾶσα ἁμαρτίαν ἀνομωτέρους. Cf. Epistle of Barnabas, c. v.

[3] H. E. III. 25, 4 : ἐν δὲ τοῖς νόθοις κατατετάχθω καὶ τῶν Παύλου πράξεων γραφή, ὅ τε λεγόμενος Ποιμὴν, καὶ ἡ ἀποκάλυψις Πέτρου, καὶ πρὸς τούτοις ἡ φερομένη Βαρνάβα ἐπιστολὴ, καὶ τῶν ἀποστόλων αἱ λεγόμεναι διδαχαί.

epistle for the edification of the Church, which is read among the apocryphal scriptures.[1]

Whence it was remarked by Pearson[2] that, though Jerome believed the epistle to have been written by S. Barnabas, he did not accept it as part of the New Testament.

The epistle of S. Barnabas does not possess many claims to interest, apart from its extreme antiquity. Though accepted in the very earliest period as the work of the companion of S. Paul, and quoted frequently as such by Clement of Alexandria and Origen, it was even by Eusebius classed among the spurious books; and when the tendency to accept books of this class as genuine is considered, the fact of its condemnation at so early a period may be considered decisive, unless strong internal evidence to the contrary can be produced. Such there does not appear to be, the contents of the epistle offering but little clue to its authorship. It must have been written after the capture of Jerusalem,[3] and the quotations in Clement of Alexandria make it evident that it was compiled before 150 A.D. The date consequently falls between 70 and 150 A.D., and as the work is not quoted by Irenæus, the later part of the period seems the most plausible. Its claims to regard seem

[1] DeViris Illustr. c. 6 (Opp. ed. Vallars. II. 839): "Barnabas Cyprius qui et Joseph Levites, cum Paulo gentium apostolus ordinatus, unam ad aedificationem ecclesiae pertinentem epistolam composuit quae inter apocryphas scripturas legitur."

[2] Vindic. Ignat., p. 1, 4.

[3] Cap. xvi. cf. Hefele Prolegom. p. xiii.

certainly smaller than those of any other writer in the collection. The recent recovery of the original Greek text in the Codex Sinaiticus has, however, invested it with a certain interest which the Latin translation, by which it had hitherto been known, did not possess. It was most probably composed at Alexandria. The main argument of the epistle attributed to S. Barnabas is that the Jews are mistaken in the interpretation of their law, which they interpret literally, whereas its real meaning was of an ethical and mystical character; the prohibition of different kind of animals for instance not having been intended to be interpreted literally (cap. x.), but referring to different kinds of men resembling the character of unclean animals which are to be avoided. The style of treatment is extremely fanciful, and the argument scarcely needs repetition.[1]

[1] He seems to have concluded that because the Old Testament contains a certain amount of typical teaching, the brazen serpent to which he refers in lxv. being an acknowledged type of our Lord, the whole of the Old Testament was allegorical and figurative, and that this was not known to the Jews, though it was, apparently, to Moses and the prophets, the true signification of the Jewish dispensation being revealed to Christians. This he attempts to prove by numerous quotations from the Old Testament and the Apocryphal books. The attempt to apply a mystical interpretation to the Jewish ceremonial law is peculiarly unfortunate, because the Jews had, besides, a moral law of their own, and did not need a mystical interpretation of the ceremonial law. The work is pervaded by a spirit of sincere piety, and the writer was well acquainted with the Old Testament Scriptures, though often quoting very

The epistle contains numerous quotations from the Septuagint version of the Old Testament, which are, however, extremely inaccurate, and has a saying ascribed to our Lord which is not found in the New Testament: "As the Lord saith, Let us resist all iniquity, and hate it."[1] This quotation is not, however, found in the Greek text.

There is also an interesting allusion to the observance of Sunday,[2] one of the earliest if not the very earliest in the ecclesiastical writers: "Wherefore we keep the eighth day as a day of joy, on which Jesus rose from the dead, and after he had appeared, ascended into heaven."

loosely. The epistle cannot, however, be considered to have any theological value, and it is only its extreme antiquity and its traditional connection with the name of S. Barnabas, whose name, however, does not occur in the course of it (nor does that of any other contemporary name), that entitle it to notice.

[1] Cap. iv. "Sicut dixit filius Dei, Resistamus omni iniquitati et odio habeamus eam." Cf. James iv. 7 ; II. Tim. xvi. 19; Ps. cxix. 163. In cap. vii. ad fin. is a passage which is most probably a loose quotation from Matt. xvi. 24.

[2] Cap. xv. For the history of the religious observance of the first day of the week cf. the following passages :— John xx. 26 ; Acts xx. 7 ; I. Cor. xvi. 12 ; Revel. i. 10 ; where the expression κυριακὴ ἡμέρα first occurs. In the epistle of S. Ignatius to the Magnesians, cap. 9, the observance of the Lord's Day as a substitute for the Sabbath is mentioned. Justin Martyr is the first who mentions the Greek equivalent for Sunday (Τῇ τοῦ ἡλίου λεγομένῃ ἡμέρᾳ). Apol. Prim. c. 89). It is called *Dies Dominica* and *Dies Solis* in Tertullian (Apol. cxvi. ; De Cor. cap. 3.) Cf. also Irenæus Frag. viii. (Stieren). Dionysius of Corinth, quoted by Eusebius, H. E. iv. 13, 11.

The Epistles of Ignatius.

NOTHING appears to be known with any certainty about the birth or personal history of Ignatius, except that he was, Bishop of Antioch towards the close of the first century. Whether he was a Greek, or a Syrian, or a native of Sardinia, or a Phrygian, has been made a matter of controversy. Questions have also been raised as to whether he was a disciple of S. Peter, or of S. Paul, or of S. John. There seems to be little doubt that he had conversed with the Apostles, but apparently had never seen our Lord. The title of Theophorus, which he adopted, and which he himself explained to mean one who has Christ in his heart—literally deific, or a bearer of God—was by a curious mistake translated by some of the Greeks passively, "borne by God;" and from hence the legend seems to have arisen that Ignatius was the little child whom our Lord took in his arms when he rebuked the contention of the disciples.

The length of his episcopate and the events that marked it do not seem to be known. The circumstances of his martyrdom are, however, well established. The Emperor Trajan, A.D. 107 or 115, for there is a controversy about the exact date, while making an expedition against Armenia and the Parthians, stayed for a while at Antioch. During his stay there Ignatius was brought before him, and was, by his orders, conveyed to Rome to be devoured by wild beasts, guarded by ten soldiers, whom he calls ten leopards. He was conveyed to Rome by a long and dangerous route, partly by land and partly by sea. Landing at last at Portus, at the mouth of the Tiber, he was thence conveyed to Rome, and on the 20th of December thrown to the wild beasts in the amphitheatre. He is said to have been devoured by the lions, who left only the harder bones of his body; these were collected by his friends and sent to Antioch, where they were first interred in the cemetery outside the gate, and afterwards removed by the Emperor Theodosius II. to the church of S. Ignatius.

Ignatius, during his journey from Antioch to Rome, was allowed to communicate with the Christians in the various towns through which he passed; and he is said in the course of his journey to have written a number of epistles. That he actually wrote epistles is a fact beyond controversy, as it is attested by his contemporary Polycarp, who, however, gives no particulars, either about the time at which they were written, or the persons to whom they were addressed. A passage from one of the existing epistles is also quoted by Irenæus, whose date is but little removed from Ignatius. He is also quoted by Origen. This seems to be all in the matter that is beyond the reach of controversy; how much of the real Ignatius has come down to us being a matter of great doubt.[1]

[1] Polyc. Ep. ad Philipp. c. xiii. Iren. adv. Hær. v. 28,

At the revival of learning fifteen letters professing to be by Ignatius were discovered and printed. Three of them existed only in Latin. They were an epistle to S. John, a second epistle to S. John, and an epistle to the Blessed Virgin. They appeared in Paris, 1495, and form the first portion of the Ignatian literature that appeared in print. The volume which contained this contained also a letter of the Blessed Virgin to S. John, and a life of Thomas à Beckett. These three epistles have long been acknowledged to be spurious.

There remain twelve epistles, which exist both in Latin and Greek; of them seven are enumerated by Eusebius and Jerome, and are consequently, and with justice, considered to possess greater claim to authenticity than the remaining five. These seven epistles, which are all that can fairly claim to have come from the pen of S. Ignatius, are addressed to six Christian Churches, and one to S. Polycarp. Unfortunately, the question is by no means decided by taking the list of Eusebius[1] as the criterion of the genuineness of the Ignatian

quotes the epistle of Ignatius to the Romans, c. iv. Origen, proleg. in Cantic. tom. iii. p. 30, also quotes the epistle to the Romans, cap. iv. Compare Eusebius, Eccles. Hist. iii. 36.

[1] The seven mentioned by Eusebius are: To the Smyrnæans, to Polycarp, to the Ephesians, to the Magnesians, to the Philadelphians, to the Trallians, to the Romans. The eight others are: One to the Virgin Mary, two to the Apostle John, one to Mary of Cassobelæ, one to the Tarsians, one to the Antiochians, one to Hero of Antioch, one to the Philippians.

remains. Of these seven epistles there exist two recensions, one considerably longer than the other, and an ancient Latin version to correspond. It is evident that both of these recensions could not have come from the pen of Ignatius, and the shorter recension was generally received as the best representation of what he wrote, the longer being regarded as interpolated.[1] The shorter recension of the Ignatian epistles made its appearance in the middle of the seventeenth century, and the controversy on the subject might possibly have soon subsided had not a fresh element been imported into it. The epistles of Ignatius are, it is well known, both in the shorter and longer recensions, full of praise of the episcopal office. The bishop is represented in language which is certainly stronger than that used either in the New Testament or in the remains of the Apostolic period, as the person of highest importance in the Christian Church. Nothing is to be done without him; he is the centre of the whole ecclesiastical polity. Now in the middle of the seventeenth century there existed a number of persons, many of

[1] It is impossible, in a work of this kind, to enter at length into any account of the Ignatian controversy, which has lasted from the beginning of the seventeenth century to the present day. The epistles have been attacked on various grounds, partly as containing references to events later than the date of Ignatius, partly as containing things that Ignatius was unlikely to have written. A good modern account is found in the Introduction to Cureton's "Corpus Ignatianum." Cf. also Hefele's Prolegomena.

considerable learning, whose admiration for the episcopal office was by no means excessive, and who found it difficult to believe that a friend and companion of the Apostles could have written in praise of a form of Church government which they considered to be erroneous. The Presbyterian party, both in England and abroad, consequently attacked with great vigour the genuineness of the Ignatian epistles. Dr. John Owen, in England, and De Saumain and Daillé, on the Continent, assailed the epistles; the latter, it is always acknowledged, with great ability and learning. The work of Daillé had the effect of bringing out Pearson's celebrated work, the "Vindiciæ Ignatianæ," which appeared in 1672, and was generally considered to have established the genuineness of the shorter recension. The Presbyterian controversy subsided with the abolition of the English Commonwealth, and the question as to the genuineness of Ignatius seemed to be laid finally at rest. Suspicions, however, were always entertained that even the shorter recension had been more or less interpolated, especially in regard to the passages in which the importance of Episcopacy is described.

In the present century a fresh element has been imported into the question. In 1843, Archdeacon Tattam discovered in the library of the Syrian convent in the desert of Nitria, in Egypt, a Syriac version of the epistles of S. Ignatius to the Ephesians, to the Romans, and to S. Polycarp. This version, which is of great antiquity, is considerably shorter than even the short recension of the Greek, and omits the chief passages which formed the ground of former attacks upon the genuineness of the remains. They were published by Dr. Cureton in 1845; and in an interesting volume, in which he followed up his discovery ("Corpus Ignatianum"), he endeavoured to prove, not only that the authority of the Syriac version of these three was superior to any of the Greek recensions, but that it comprised all that could with safety be ascribed to Ignatius. This assertion naturally produced a fresh controversy. Hefele,[1] one of the latest editors of the Apostolic Fathers, maintains that the Syriac version was merely an epitome made for devotional purposes by a Syrian[2] monk,

---

[1] Hefele, Patres Apostolici. Prolegom. p. 61.

[2] The fact that the Syriac version of the epistles of Ignatius does not contain passages that were supposed to throw a doubt upon the authenticity of the epistles renders it probable that it represents the text in a state more nearly resembling the original than either of the Greek recensions, bearing, in fact, to the shorter Greek text the same relation which the latter bears to the longer and interpolated text. It is scarcely conceivable that a writer making an epitome of the longer works should have omitted the passages which modern criticism would assign to a later date than that of Ignatius; but it seems too much to conclude that these three epistles are the only genuine works of Ignatius. They form part of manuscripts which contain other works chiefly of a devotional character. As the other works they contain are selections from larger works, so these three epistles of Ignatius may not unnaturally be a selection of that which the compiler judged most suitable for his purpose. It seems

who had left out the passages which he deemed unsuitable for his purpose. The late Baron Bunsen[1] supported the view of Dr. Cureton, which is apparently accepted by Professor Max Muller.[2]

Thus, a fresh element of doubt has been imported into the controversy, and it would be too much to say that the question is by any means settled; it apparently awaits the discovery of fresh Syriac manuscripts, two only having as yet been discovered containing the three epistles.

hardly too much to expect that further researches among the libraries of the Eastern monasteries might result in the discovery of shorter versions of the other epistles recognized by Eusebius.

[1] Hippolytus and His Age, I, 98. Analecta Ante-Nicæa, I, 34.

[2] Article on Bunsen in vol. iii. of Collected Essays, p. 38.

The Epistle of Polycarp.

OF Polycarp, Bishop of Smyrna, little is known, except the circumstances of his martyrdom, of which an ancient account has been preserved in a letter from the Church of Smyrna to the Church of the Philomelians. Of the antiquity of this account there is no question, as it is quoted by Eusebius;[1] but whether it is really a contemporary account of the martyrdom, and whether, if so, it is trustworthy, is a matter of considerable controversy, mainly on account of several extraordinary circumstances that were said to have attended the martyrdom, and which have given rise to the suspicion that they were the invention of a later period. There does not, however, seem any means for arriving at a decision as to the authority of the Martyrdom of Polycarp; it is at any rate the account which even prior to the time of Eusebius was received of the event; as to the credibility or not of the circumstances the reader must judge for himself. With the exception of the passage, which may be a corrupt reading, representing the rising of a dove from the side of Polycarp,[2] there is nothing in the account absolutely

---

[1] Hist. Eccl. iv. 15. Cf. Hefele's Prolegomena, p. 83.

[2] Cap. xvi. ἐξῆλθε περιστερὰ καὶ πλῆθος αἵματος. The passage might be rejected on purely critical grounds, as it is not found in Eusebius, and is omitted in two manuscripts. Cf. Jacobson's Patres Apostolici, ii. p. 645. Various con-

supernatural; though there is much that is evidently due to the excited imagination of those who, with great peril to themselves, were witnessing the death of their Bishop.

There are, however, several circumstances connected with Polycarp which render him extremely interesting as an ecclesiastical character. He is supposed, to have been the angel of the Church of Smyrna[1] to whom S. John addressed a portion of the Apocalypse. He was Bishop of Smyrna when Ignatius passed through the city, and he has left an epistle of undoubted authenticity, containing some of the earliest quotations from the New Testament. The date of his martyrdom is in all probability between 160 and 170 A.D.[2] He thus is quite the latest of the

<small>jectures have been made on the supposition that the passage is corrupt: ἐπ ἀριστερά, on the left; περὶ στερνὰ, about the breast; περὶ στύρακα, about the haft of the spear: or, merely that the word περιστερὰ had been inserted on the margin as a pious ejaculation of the copyist, and had afterwards found its way into the text. The latter explanation is preferred by Jacobson and Hefele, whose notes may be consulted.

[1] There seems to be little doubt that he was appointed to the Bishopric of Smyrna by S. John: cf. Tertullian de Præscript. 32; Jerome de Viris. Illust. 17. That he was the Angel of the Church of Smyrna mentioned in the Revelations seems probable enough, but is not universally accepted. Cf. Hefele's Prolégomena, p. lxxv.

[2] Various dates have been assigned, between 147 and 178 A.D. The best authorities put it between 165 and 170 A.D. (Tillemont, 166; Gieseler and Neander, 167; Baronius and</small>

Apostolic Fathers, outliving S. Clement by more than half a century, and Ignatius by more than thirty or forty years. He must have conversed with the Apostles, and that he did so there is no doubt, when he was in extreme youth, and they in old age. He consequently carries the Apostolic tradition into the second century, and forms the link between Irenæus, who had never seen the Apostles, but had conversed with Polycarp, and in whom we pass out of the Apostolic Fathers into the ecclesiastical writers, and the Apostles themselves, whose personal identity and historical character is thus satisfactorily established. It is to Irenæus that we naturally turn for information about his teacher, and several interesting passages are found on the subject. In the epistle to Florinus, quoted by Eusebius,[1] he thus writes: "For I saw thee while yet a boy in lower Asia, by the side of Polycarp, distinguishing thyself in the royal palace, and endeavouring to win his favour. For I remember the things that happened then better than the things that happened lately; for the things that we have learnt in boyhood, growing with our growth, remain in the mind, so that I can even describe the very place in which the blessed Polycarp sat and discoursed; his goings out and comings in; the character of his

---

Mosheim, 169. Cf. Hefele's Prolegomena, p. lxvii; Robertson's Church History, vol. i. p. 29, note D.

[1] Eccles. Hist., v. 20.

life and the form of his body, and the discourse which he had with the multitude; and how he used to narrate his intercourse with S. John and the rest of the Apostles who had seen the Lord, and how he used to mention their words, and what the things were that he had heard from them concerning the Lord and concerning his mighty works and his teaching. All these things Polycarp having received from eye witnesses of the life of the Lord, used to narrate in harmony with the Scriptures."[1]

And again: "Polycarp not only having been taught by the Apostles, and having conversed with many who had seen Christ, but also having been appointed bishop by the Apostles in the Church in Smyrna, in Asia, whom we have also seen in early youth, for he continued a long time, and in extreme old age, having gloriously and nobly undergone martyrdom, departed out of life, having always taught the things that he had heard from the Apostles, which all the Church handed down, and which are also true. To them all the Churches of Asia bear witness, and those who have up to this time succeeded Polycarp, who is a far more trustworthy and safe witness of truth then Valentinus and Marcion, and the rest of the perverts. Polycarp, when visiting Anicetus at Rome, converted to the Church of God many of the aforesaid heretics, preaching that he had received from the Apostles, even that which was handed down by the Church.

---

[1] Iren. Adv. Hær., iii. 3. Euseb. Eccles. Hist., iv. 14.

And there are some who have heard him say that John the disciple of the Lord, when at Ephesus, and going to bathe, finding Cerinthus within, hurried out of the bath without having washed, exclaiming 'Let us fly lest the bath should fall down, since Cerinthus, the enemy of truth, is within.' And Polycarp trembled when Marcion once met him, and said, Dost thou know me? and replied, 'I know thee to be the first born of Satan.'"

In another passage, Irenæus describes the intercourse between Polycarp and Anicetus, Bishop of Rome, whom Polycarp had visited to settle the dispute between the Eastern and Western Church as to the proper period of keeping Easter. They were unable to agree, and had differences on some other small points which are not mentioned, but parted on friendly terms:[1] an interesting illustration of the fact that the Church of Rome at that period did not claim authority in matters of faith. "Neither Anicetus could persuade Polycarp," Irenæus observes with great simplicity," "nor Polycarp, Anicetus." The two Bishops, however, communicated together, and Polycarp apparently officiated in the Church of Anicetus.

[1] There is some dispute as to the exact meaning of the words of Irenæus, cf. Stieren's Irenæus, vol. i. p. 827, but they no doubt imply very friendly union in a public service. καὶ τούτων οὕτως ἐχόντων ἐκοινώνησαν ἑαυτοῖς, καὶ ἐν τῇ ἐκκλησίᾳ παρεχώρησεν ὁ Ἀνίκητος τὴν εὐχαριστίαν τῇ Πολυκάρπῳ, κατ' ἐντροπὴν δηλονότι, καὶ μετ' εἰρήνης ἀπ' ἀλλήλων ἀπηλλάγησαν.

[2] Iren. Fragment, iii. Stieren. Euseb. H. E. v. 24.

Beyond these statements of Irenæus, we seem to have little trustworthy information about Polycarp, though the place has been abundantly supplied by tradition. The authenticity of his epistle to the Philippians has been attacked by Daillé and others; but it is confirmed by the complete chain of evidence extending from the time of Irenæus,[1] his contemporary, who mentions that Polycarp wrote epistles to neighbouring Churches, and expressly quotes the epistle to the Philippians. "There is," he says, "a most powerful epistle of Polycarp to the Philippians, from which they who will, and who care for their own salvation, can learn the character of his faith and his preaching of the truth."[2]

The Greek text of the epistle is unfortunately imperfect, cap. x—xiv. being supplied from an ancient Latin version. The epistle was first published at Paris in Latin, A.D. 1498. A collation of the chief manuscript authorities is given in Jacobson's Patres Apostolici; cf. Hefele's Prolegomena, p. lxxxi.

---

[1] Epist. to Florinus. Euseb. Hist. Eccles. v. 20.
[2] Iren. adv. Hær. iii. 3. Euseb. Hist. Eccles. iv. 14.

The Martyrdom of Ignatius.

The account of the martyrdom of Ignatius, though received as genuine by scholars of a past date, such as Ussher, Dodwell, Pearson, and Cotelier, is not accepted by modern scholars[1] as a contemporary account. No quotation from it is found in the writings of the first six centuries,[2] nor is there any allusion during that period to its existence as an independent work. It, however, agrees with the account of Eusebius and S. John Chrysostom respecting the martyrdom of Ignatius, and contains nothing absolutely irreconcilable with the ordinary history of Trajan, though there is some question as to the date of the martyrdom, which the Greek version puts in the ninth, the Latin in the fourth year of Trajan. The some-

[1] Its genuineness is rejected by Neander, ii. 443; Bunsen, "Hippolytus and His Age," i. 89; Davidson's "Introduction to the New Testament," ii. 369. It is, however, defended by Hefele (Prolegomena to Ignatius), who accepts the whole account as genuine; Ussher, Grotius, and others acknowledging a certain amount of interpolation in the latter part. A Syriac version brought from the library at Bagdad by G. Rich has been edited by Dr. Cureton; it is apparently translated from the Greek, from which it differs but little. Two interesting dissertations on the subject by Smith and Pearson are given in Bishop Jacobson's Patres Apostolici, p. 558. Jacobson accepts it with some hesitation, acknowledging the latter part to be spurious. Patres Apostolici, ii. 598.

[2] It is first alluded to by Evagrius, H. E. I. 10.

what harsh sentence of Bunsen, that it is "an unhistorical and forged document," might be represented more gently in the form that it conveys to us the traditional account of the martyrdom of S. Ignatius, in all probability not differing very widely from the truth, though the account as we have it did not, in all probability, assume its present form much before the sixth century. It exists in Greek, probably the original, Latin, and Syriac, and was supposed to have been drawn up by Philo and Agathopus, two deacons, one of the Church of Antioch, the other of Tarsus, whom Ignatius mentions in his epistles to the Smyrnæans and Philadelphians. The Greek was first edited by Archbishop Ussher, in 1647.

The Epistles of S. Clement.

		Page
1st Clement to Corinthians		3
2nd Clement — do —		52
Barnabas		67
Ignatius (General)		105
Ignatius to Magnesians		116
Ignatius to Trallians		121
1. Ignatius to Romans		127
Ignatius to Philadelphians		136
Ignatius to Smyrneans		143
1. Ignatius to Polycarp		157
Polycarp to Philadelphians		159
2. Ignatius to Polycarp		199
Ignatius to Ephesians		203
2. Ignatius to Romans		206
(Shepherd of Hermas)		

The First Epistle of S. Clement to the Corinthians.

THE Church of God which sojourneth at Rome, to the Church of God which sojourneth at Corinth, to them that are called and sanctified in the will of God through our Lord Jesus Christ: Grace and peace be multiplied unto you from God Almighty through Jesus Christ.

I.

On account of the sudden and repeated calamities and mischances, brethren, that have come upon us, we suppose that we have the more slowly given heed to the things that are disputed among you, beloved, and to the foul and unholy sedition, alien and foreign to the elect of God, which a few headstrong and self-willed persons have kindled to such a degree of madness, that your venerable and famous name, worthy to be loved of all men, is greatly blasphemed. For who that hath tarried among you hath not approved your most virtuous and firm faith, hath not admired your sober and seemly piety in Christ, hath not proclaimed your splendid disposition of hospitality, hath not deemed blessed your perfect and unerring knowledge? For ye did all things without respect of persons, and walked in the laws of God, submitting yourselves to them that have the rule over you, and giving the due honour to the presbyters that are among you. Young men ye enjoined to think such things as be sober and grave. Women ye exhorted to perform all things in a blameless and honourable and pure conscience, loving dutifully their own husbands; and ye taught them to manage the affairs of their houses with gravity, keeping in the rule of obedience, being temperate in all things.

II.

And ye were all humble, boasting of nothing, submitting yourselves rather than subjecting others, more gladly giving than receiving, content with the provision that God had given you; and attending diligently to his words, ye received them into your very hearts, and his sufferings were before your eyes. Thus a deep and rich peace was given to all, and an insatiable longing for doing good; and a plentiful outpouring of the Holy Spirit was upon all of you. And ye, being filled with a holy desire, with excellent zeal and pious confidence, stretched out your arms to God Almighty, beseeching him to be merciful unto you, if ye had in anything unwillingly done amiss. Ye contended day and night for the whole brotherhood, that in his mercy and good pleasure the number of his elect might be saved. Ye were simple and sincere without malice one toward another: all sedition and all schism were abominable unto you. Ye grieved over the transgressions of your neighbour, judging his shortcomings your own. Ye repented for no good deed, being ready to every good work; and being adorned with a very virtuous and holy habit of life, ye did all things in his fear. The commandments and ordinances of the Lord were written on the breadth of your heart.

III.

All honour and enlargement was given to you, and thus was fulfilled that which is written:—The beloved ate and drank, and was enlarged and grew fat and kicked. From this came emulation and envy, strife and sedition, persecution and disorder, war and captivity. Thus the mean men were lifted up against the honourable; those of no repute against those of good repute; the foolish against the wise; the young against the elder. Through this justice and peace are afar off, because each of you leaveth off the fear of God and is dimsighted in his faith, nor walketh in the laws of his commandments, nor behaveth as becometh a citizen of Christ; but each walketh according to his own evil lusts, having taken up unjust and unholy envy, by which also death entered into the world.

IV.

For it is thus written: And it came to pass after certain days, that Cain brought of the fruit of the ground a sacrifice to God, and Abel brought also of the firstlings of the flock and of their fat. And God had respect to Abel and to his gifts; but to Cain and his gifts he had no regard. And Cain was grieved greatly, and his countenance fell. And God said unto Cain, Why art thou very sorrowful, and why hath thy countenance fallen? If thou hast rightly offered, but hast not rightly divided, hast thou not sinned? Hold thy peace; thy gift returneth unto thee, and thou shalt be master over it. And Cain said unto Abel, Let us pass over into the field. And it came to pass while they were in the field, Cain rose up against Abel his brother and slew him. See, brethren, jealousy and envy wrought the slaughter of a brother. Through envy our father Jacob fled from the face of his brother Esau. Envy caused Joseph to be persecuted unto death, and to enter into bondage. Envy compelled Moses to flee from the face of Pharaoh, king of Egypt, because he heard his countryman say, Who made thee a judge or a juror over us? Wilt thou kill me, as thou didst the Egyptian yesterday? Through envy Aaron and Miriam pitched their tents without the camp. Envy brought down Dathan and Abiram alive to the grave, because they contended against Moses, the servant of

God. Through envy David suffered jealousy not only of foreigners, but was persecuted also by Saul, king of Israel.

V.

But let us pass from ancient examples, and come unto those who have in these last times wrestled for the faith. Let us take the noble examples of our own generation. Through jealousy and envy the greatest and most just pillars of the Church were persecuted, and came even unto death. Let us place before our eyes the good Apostles. Peter, through unjust envy, endured not one or two but many labours, and at last, having delivered his testimony, departed unto the place of glory due to him. Through envy Paul, too, showed by example the prize that is given to patience: seven times was he cast into chains; he was banished; he was stoned; having become a herald, both in the East and in the West, he obtained the noble renown due to his faith; and having preached righteousness to the whole world, and having come to the extremity of the West, and having borne witness before rulers, he departed at length out of the world, and went to the holy place, having become the greatest example of patience.

VI.

To these men, who walked in holiness, there was gathered a great multitude of the elect, who, having suffered, through envy, many insults and tortures, became a most excellent example among us. Through envy women were persecuted, even the Danaides and Dircæ, who, after enduring dreadful and unholy insults, attained to the sure course of the faith; and they who were weak in body received a noble reward. Envy hath estranged the minds of wives from their husbands, and changed the saying of our father Adam: This is now bone of my bone, and flesh of my flesh. Envy and strife have overthrown mighty cities and rooted out great nations.

VII.

These things we enjoin you, beloved, not only by way of admonition to you, but as putting ourselves also in mind. For we are in the same arena, and the same contest is imposed upon us. Wherefore, let us leave empty and vain cares, and come unto the glorious and venerable rule of our holy calling. Let us consider what is good and pleasing and acceptable before him who made us. Let us look steadfastly to the blood of Christ, and see how precious in the sight of God is his blood, which having been poured out for our salvation, brought to the whole world the grace of repentance. Let us go back to all generations, and learn that in every generation God hath granted a place for repentance to such as wished to return into him. Noah preached repentance, and as many as hearkened unto him were saved. Jonah prophesied destruction to the Ninevites, and they,

VIII.

The ministers of the grace of God spake by the Holy Spirit concerning repentance; and the Lord of all himself spake concerning repentance with an oath. As I live, saith the Lord, I desire not the death of a sinner, as I desire his repentance; adding thereto an excellent saying: Repent, O house of Israel, from your iniquity: Say unto the sons of my people, Though your sins reach from earth to heaven, and though they be redder than scarlet, and blacker than sackcloth, and ye turn unto me with your whole heart and say, My father, I will hearken unto you as to an holy people. And in another place he speaketh in this wise: Wash, and be ye clean; take away the wickedness from your souls from before my eyes; cease from your evil deeds, learn to do well; seek judgment; deliver him that is oppressed; give judgment for the orphan, and justify the widow; and come and let us reason together, saith the Lord; and though your sins be as purple, I will make them white as snow; and though they be as scarlet, I will make them white as wool. And if ye be willing and hearken unto me, ye shall eat the good things of the earth; but if ye be not willing, and hearken not, the sword shall devour you. The mouth of the Lord hath said this. Desiring, therefore, that all his beloved ones should partake of repentance, he hath confirmed it by his almighty will.

IX.

Wherefore, let us submit ourselves to his excellent and glorious will, and, becoming suppliants of his mercy and goodness, let us fall before him and betake ourselves to his mercies, laying aside vain labour and strife, and envy that leadeth to death. Let us look steadfastly at those that have ministered with perfectness to his excellent glory. Let us take as example Enoch, who, having been found just by reason of obedience, was translated, and death came not upon him. Noah, having been found faithful, preached, by his ministry, regeneration unto the world, and by him God preserved the animals that entered with one consent into the ark.

X.

Abraham, who was called the friend, was found faithful, inasmuch as he became obedient to the words of God. This man, by obedience, went out from his land and his kinsfolk, and the house of his father, that, by leaving a scanty country and weak kinsfolk and a small house, he might inherit the promise of God. For he saith unto him, Go out from thy land and thy kinsfolk, and the house of thy father, and I will make thee a great nation, and bless thee, and magnify thy name, and thou shalt be blessed; and I will bless them that bless thee, and

Gen. xii. 1, 3.

curse them that curse thee, and in thee shall all
the tribes of the earth be blessed. And again,
when he separated from Lot, God said unto him,
Lift up thine eyes, and look from the place where Gen. xiii. 14.
thou now art unto the north and unto the south, 16.
and unto the east and unto the sea; for all the land
which thou seest, to thee will I give it and to thy
seed for ever, and I will make thy seed as the
dust of the earth: if any man can number the
dust of the earth, thy seed also shall be numbered.
And again he saith, God brought forth Abraham, Gen xv 5. 6
and said unto him: Look up to heaven and num-
ber the stars, if thou art able to number them, for
so shall thy seed be. And Abraham believed God,
and it was counted to him for righteousness.
Through faith and hospitality a son was given
unto him in old age, and through obedience he
offered him a sacrifice unto God in one of the
mountains that he showed him.

XI.

By hospitality and godliness Lot was saved out
of Sodom when the whole region round about was
judged with fire and brimstone ; the Lord making
it manifest that he leaveth not them that hope upon
him, but appointeth to punishment and torment
them that turn in another away. For his wife, who
went out together with him, being of another mind,
and not being in concord with him, was on that
account placed as a sign, so that she became a

pillar of salt even to this day; that it might be known to all that the double-minded, and they who doubt concerning the power of God, are for a judgment and a sign to all generations.

XII.

Through faith and hospitality Rahab the harlot was saved; for when spies were sent unto Jericho by Jesus, the son of Nun, the king of the land knew that they had come to spy out his country, and sent out men to apprehend them that they might be taken and put to death. But the hospitable Rahab having received them, hid them in an upper story under the stalks of flax. When, therefore, the men from the king came upon her, and said, There came unto thee men who are spies of this our land; bring them out, for the king so commanded it; she answered, The two men of whom ye speak came unto me, but they departed quickly and are on their way; but she showed not the men unto them. And she said unto the men, Of a surety I know that the Lord your God has given over this city unto you; for the fear and trembling of you hath fallen upon them that inhabit it; when, therefore, it hath happened unto you to take it, save me and the house of my father. And they said unto her, So shall it be, even as thou hast spoken unto us. When, therefore, thou knowest that we are come, thou shalt gather together all thy household under thy roof, and they shall be saved; but as many as shall be found without the house shall be destroyed. And they proceeded further to give her a sign, that she should hang from her house scarlet, making it manifest beforehand that through the blood of the Lord is redemption to all who believe and hope upon God. Behold, beloved, how there was not only faith, but prophecy in the woman.

XIII.

Let us therefore, brethren, be humble, laying aside all boasting and pride, and folly and wrath, and let us do that which is written; for the Holy Spirit saith, Let not the wise boast in his wisdom, Jer. ix. 23 nor the strong in his strength, nor the rich in his riches; but let him that boasteth make his boast in the Lord even by seeking him and doing judgment and justice. Let us especially remember the words of our Lord Jesus Christ which he spake when teaching gentleness and long-suffering: Show Matt. viii. 1, mercy, that ye may obtain mercy; forgive, that it Luke vi. 36, may be forgiven unto you; as ye do, so shall it 38. be done unto you; as ye give, so shall it be given unto you; as ye judge, so shall ye be judged; as ye are kindly affectioned, so shall kindness be showed unto you; with whatsoever measure ye measure, with the same shall it be measured unto you. With this commandment and with this exhortation let us strengthen ourselves, that we may walk obedient to his holy words with all humility. For the Holy Scripture saith, Upon whom shall I have respect but upon him that is meek and quiet, and that trembleth at my words?

<small>Isaiah lxvi. 2.</small>

XIV.

It is therefore meet and right, men and brethren, that we should be obedient unto God rather than follow them that be leaders in the pride and disorderliness of detestable envy. For we shall incur no slight harm, but rather a great danger, if we rashly give ourselves up to the wills of men who launch out into strife and sedition to estrange us from that which is good. Let us, therefore, show kindness towards them according to the mercy and sweetness of him that made us. For it is written, The men of kindness shall inherit the land. The innocent shall be left upon it; but they that be lawless shall be destroyed out of it. And again he saith, I saw the unrighteous man exalted on high and lifted up like the cedars of Lebanon. I passed by, and behold he was not; I sought his place and found it not. Keep innocence, and regard righteousness; for there is a remnant that remaineth to the man of peace.

<small>Prov. ii. 21.</small>

<small>Ps. xxxvii. 36, 38.</small>

XV.

Let us therefore cleave unto them who live in peace and godliness, not unto them who hypocritically profess to desire peace. For he saith in a certain place, This people honoureth me with

<small>Isaiah xxix. 13.</small>

their lips, but their heart is far from me. And again, With their mouth did they bless, but with their heart did they curse. And again he saith, They loved him with their mouth, and with their tongue they lied against him. For their heart was not right with him, nor were they faithful in his covenant. Let the crafty lips be put to silence, and may the Lord destroy the haughty tongue, even they who said, Let us magnify our tongue, our lips are our own; who is master over us? On account of the misery of the poor, and on account of the groaning of the needy, I will now arise, saith the Lord; I will set him in safety, I will deal confidently with him.

XVI.

For Christ belongeth unto them that are humble, not unto them that exalt themselves over his flock. Our Lord Jesus Christ, who is the sceptre of the majesty of God, came not in the arrogance of boasting and pride, though he was able to do so; but in humility, even as the Holy Spirit spake concerning him. For he saith, Lord, who hath believed our report, and to whom hath the arm of the Lord been revealed? Like a child have we delivered our message before him; he is as a root in a thirsty land. There is no form nor glory in him, and we beheld him, and he had neither form nor comeliness, but his form was despised, lacking comeliness, beyond the form of the sons of men.

He was a man stricken and in toil, knowing how to bear infirmity, for his face was turned away; it was dishonoured and held in no reputation. He beareth our sins and suffereth pain on our account, and we esteemed him as one in toil, stricken and afflicted. He was wounded for our sins, and for our transgressions did he suffer infirmity; the chastisement of our peace was upon him, and by his stripes we are healed. All we, like sheep, have gone astray, every one hath wandered into his own way, and the Lord hath given him up for our sins; and he, through affliction, openeth not his mouth. He was led like a lamb to the slaughter, and as a sheep before its shearers is dumb, so openeth he not his mouth. In his humiliation his judgment was taken away, and who shall declare his generation, for his life is taken from the earth; for the iniquity of my people he hath come unto death. And I will give the wicked in requital for his tomb and the rich for his death: for he did no sin, neither was guile found in his mouth: and the Lord willeth to purify him from stripes. If ye make an offering for sin your soul shall prolong its days. And the Lord willeth to take away from the travail of his soul, to show him light and to form him by knowledge, to justify the righteous man who serveth many well; and their sins he shall bear himself. Wherefore he shall receive the inheritance of many, and shall divide the spoils of the strong, because his soul was delivered up unto death, and he was numbered among the transgressors, and he bore the sins of

many, and was given up for their sins. And
again he saith, I am a worm and no man—a   Ps. xxii. 6, 3
reproach of men and despised of the people : all
they who saw me mocked me, they spake with
their lips, they shook the head ; he hoped in God,
let him deliver him, let him save him, because
he desireth him. See, beloved, what an example
is given unto us ; for if the Lord so humbled
himself, what shall we do who have through his
mercy come under the yoke of his grace?

XVII.

Let us be imitators of them also who went about   Heb. xi.
in goat-skins and sheep-skins, preaching the coming
of Christ ; we mean Elias and Elisæus and Ezekiel
the prophets, and beside them those who have obtained a good report. Abraham obtained an honourable report, and was called the friend of God,
and saith, looking steadfastly to the glory of God
in humility, I am but earth and ashes. And,   Gen. xviii. 27.
moreover, concerning Job, it is thus written : Job   Job i. 1
was a just man and blameless, truthful, one that
feared God, and abstained from all evil. But he
himself, accusing himself, saith, No one is pure   Job xiv. 4.
from pollution, though his life be but for one day.
Moses was called faithful in all his house, and by
his ministry God judged his people Israel by
stripes and punishment. But he, though he was
greatly glorified, spake not haughtily, but said,
when the oracle was given him out of the bush,

XVIII.

But what shall we say of David, who obtained a good report; unto whom God said, I have found a man after my own heart, David, the son of Jesse, with my everlasting mercy have I anointed him. But he himself saith unto God, Have mercy upon me, O God, according to thy great mercy, according to the multitude of thy compassion do away with mine offences; wash me thoroughly from my iniquity, and cleanse me from my sins. For I acknowledge my iniquity, and my sin is ever before me. Against thee only have I sinned, and done this evil in thy sight, that thou mightest be justified in thy words, and overcome when thou art judged. Behold, I was shapen in wickedness, and in sin did my mother conceive me. Behold, thou hast loved truth; thou hast shown me the secret and hidden things of Thy wisdom. Thou shalt sprinkle me with hyssop, and I shall be clean. Thou shalt wash me, and I shall be whiter than snow. Thou shalt make me to hear of joy and gladness; the bones that have been humiliated shall rejoice. Turn away thy face from my sins, and blot out all my misdeeds. Create in me a new heart, O Lord, and renew a right spirit within me. Cast me not away from thy presence, and take not thy Holy Spirit from me. O give me again the joy of thy salvation, and establish me with thy guiding Spirit. I will teach sinners thy way; the ungodly shall be converted unto thee. Deliver me from blood-guiltiness, O God, thou God of my salvation; my tongue shall rejoice in thy righteousness. O Lord, thou shalt open my mouth, and my lips shall show forth thy praise. For if thou hadst desired sacrifice, I would have given it; in whole burnt offerings thou wilt not delight. The sacrifice of God is a broken spirit; a broken and a contrite heart God will not despise.

XIX.

The humility of these so-great men, who have received so good a report, and their subjection through obedience, hath made not only us but the generations before us better, namely, those who in fear and truth have received his oracles. Since, therefore, we have become the inheritors of many great and glorious actions, let us finally return to that goal of peace that was given us from the beginning; let us look steadfastly to the Father and Creator of the whole world, and let us cleave to the glorious and excellent gifts and benefits of his peace. Let us behold him in spirit, and look with the eyes of the soul to his long-suffering will. Let us consider how gentle he is toward all his creation.

XX.

*Sophocles.
Ajax, 669.*

The heavens, being put in motion by his appointment, are subject to him in peace; night and day accomplish the course ordered by him, in nothing hindering one another. The sun and the moon and the dances of the stars according to his appointment, in harmony and without any violation of order, roll on the courses appointed to them. The fruitful earth bringeth forth in due season, according to his will, abundant nourishment for men and beasts; nothing doubting, nor changing in anything from the things that are decreed by him. The unsearchable things of the abyss, and the secret ordinances of the lower parts of the earth are held together by the same command. The hollow of the vast sea, gathered together by his hand, transgresseth not the bounds placed around it; but even as he hath appointed to it, so it doeth; for *Job xxxviii. 10, 11.* he said, Thus far shalt thou come, and thy waves shall be broken within thee. The ocean, impassable to men, and the worlds that are beyond it, are governed by the same commandments of their Master. The seasons of spring and summer, autumn and winter, in peace succeed one another. The fixed stations of the winds, each in their due time, perform their services without offence. The ever-flowing fountains, made for enjoyment and health, offer their breasts without fail to sustain the lives of men. Even the smallest of animals come together in peace and harmony. All these things the great Maker and Master of all things hath appointed to be in peace and harmony, doing good unto all things, but more especially unto us, who have fled for refuge to his mercies, through our Lord Jesus Christ, to whom be glory and majesty for ever and ever. Amen.

XXI.

Beware, beloved, lest his many blessings come to be a condemnation to all of us, unless, walking worthily of him, we do what is honourable and well pleasing before him with oneness of mind. For he saith in a certain place, The spirit of the Lord is a candle, searching out the secret places of the heart. Let us see how near he is at hand, and how none of our thoughts and reasonings do escape him. Let us offend against men who are foolish, and senseless, and puffed up in the pride of their own speech, rather than against God. Let us have respect to our Lord Jesus Christ whose blood was given for us. Let us reverence them that are over us. Let us honour the elders. Let us instruct the young in the discipline of the fear of God. Let us direct our wives to that which is good; let them show forth the lovely habit of chastity, and exhibit the pure disposition of meekness. Let them make manifest in their conversation the government of their tongues; let them show love, not according to partiality, but equally to all that fear the Lord in holiness. Let your children be partakers of the discipline of Christ; let them learn how much humility availeth before God; what power a pure love hath before him; how his fear is honourable and great, preserving all who, with a pure mind, walk in holiness before him. For he is a searcher out of thoughts and counsels, his breath is in us, and when he willeth he will take it away.

XXII.

All these things doth the faith which is in Christ assure. For he himself, through the Holy Spirit, thus calleth unto us: Come, ye children, hearken unto me, I will teach you the fear of the Lord. What man is he that wisheth for life and would fain see good days? Keep thy tongue from evil, and thy lips that they speak no guile. Turn away from evil and do good; seek peace and pursue it. For the eyes of the Lord are over the just, and his ears are open to their prayer. But the face of the Lord is against them that do evil, to destroy their memorial out of the land. The righteous cried, and the Lord heard him, and delivered him out of all his troubles. Many are the afflictions of the sinner, but they that hope in the Lord, mercy shall compass them round about.

XXIII.

The Father whose mercies are over all things, who loveth to do good, hath bowels of compassion for them that fear him, and with gentleness and kindness bestoweth his favour upon them that come unto him with a pure mind. Wherefore let us not be double-minded, nor let our hearts form vain imaginations concerning his excellent and glorious gifts. Let not that Scripture be applicable unto us which saith, Wretched are the double-minded, even they that doubt in their heart and say, We have heard these things in the time of our fathers; and lo, we have grown old, and none of them hath happened unto us. O fools! compare yourselves to a tree. Take, for example, the vine: first it sheddeth its leaves, then cometh the bud, then the leaf, then the flower, after that the unripe grape, then the ripe grape. See how in a little time the fruit of the tree attaineth to maturity. Of a truth, quickly and suddenly shall his will be fulfilled; the scripture also bearing witness that he shall come quickly, and shall not tarry; and the Lord shall come suddenly into his temple, even the holy one whom ye expect.

XXIV.

Let us consider, beloved, how the Master showeth to us continually the resurrection that is about to be, of which he hath made our Lord Jesus Christ the first fruit, having raised him from the dead. Let us look, beloved, at the resurrection that is ever taking place. Day and night show to us the resurrection; the night is lulled to rest, the day ariseth; the day departeth, the night cometh on.

Let us consider the fruits, in what way a grain of corn is sown. The sower goeth forth and casteth it into the ground, and when the seeds are cast into the ground, they that fell into the ground dry and naked are dissolved; then after their dissolution, the mighty power of the providence of the Lord raiseth them up, and from one seed many grow up and bring forth fruits.

1 Cor. xv. 36.

XXV.

Let us consider the wonderful sign that happeneth in the region of the east, even about Arabia. There is a bird which is called the phœnix. This, being the only one of its kind, liveth for five hundred years. And when the time of its death draweth near, it maketh for itself a nest of frankincense and myrrh and the other perfumes, into which, when its time is fulfilled, it entereth, and then dieth. But as its flesh rotteth, a certain worm is produced, which being nourished by the moisture of the dead animal, putteth forth feathers. Then, when it hath become strong, it taketh the nest wherein are the bones of its ancestor, and bearing them, it flieth from the region of Arabia to that of Egypt, to the city which is called Heliopolis; there, in day-time, in the sight of all, it flieth up, and placeth them upon the altar of the sun, and having done so, returneth back. The priests, therefore, look into the register of the times, and find that it has come at the completion of the five-hundredth year.

Herodot. ii. 73.

XXVI.

Shall we then think it great and wonderful, if the Maker of all things shall make a resurrection of those who, in the confidence of a good faith, seek him, when even by means of a bird he showeth the greatness of his promises? For he saith in a certain place, And thou shalt raise me up, and I will give thanks unto thee; and again: I slumbered and slept; I arose up because thou art with me. And again Job saith, Thou shalt raise up this my flesh, which hath suffered all these things.

<small>Ps. xxviii. 7
Ps. iii. 5.
Ps. xxiii. 4
Job xix. 26.</small>

XXVII.

In this hope, therefore, let our souls be bound unto him who is faithful in his promises and just in his judgments. He who hath commanded men not to lie, much more shall he not lie; for nothing is impossible with God, except to lie. Let our faith, therefore, in him be kindled afresh within us, and let us consider that all things are near unto him. By the word of his majesty did he constitute all things, and by a word he is able to destroy them. Who shall say unto him, What hast thou done? or who shall resist the might of his strength? He will do all things when he willeth and as he willeth, and none of the things decreed by him shall pass away. All things are before him, and nothing hath escaped his counsel: seeing that the

<small>Heb. vi. 18.
Wisd. xii. 12.
Ps. xix. 1-3.</small>

heavens declare the glory of God, and the firmament showeth the work of his hands: day unto day uttereth speech, and night unto night proclaimeth knowledge; and there is no speech nor language where their voices are not heard.

XXVIII.

Since, therefore, all things are seen and heard of him, let us fear him and abandon the filthy desires for evil deeds, that we may be sheltered by his mercy from the judgments to come. For whither can any of us fly from his mighty hand, and what world shall receive any of them that desert from him? For the scripture saith in a certain place, Whither shall I fly, and where shall I conceal myself from thy face? If I ascend into heaven, thou art there; if I depart into the uttermost parts of the earth, there is thy right hand; if I shall make my bed in the abyss, there is thy spirit. Whither then shall we depart, and where shall we fly from him that embraceth all things?

Ps. cxxxix. 7, 10.

XXIX.

Let us, therefore, approach him with holiness of spirit, lifting unto him pure and undefiled hands; loving the kind and compassionate Father who hath made us a part of his elect. For it is thus written, When the Lord divided the nations, when he dispersed the sons of Adam, he settled the boundaries

Deut. xxxii. 8, 9.

of the nations according to the number of the
angels of God. The portion of the Lord was his
people Jacob. Israel was the lot of his inheritance.
And in another place he saith, Behold the Lord Deut. iv. 34
taketh to himself a nation from the midst of the vii. 6 ; xiv 2.
nations, even as a man taketh the first fruits of his
threshing floor; and there shall go forth from that Num. xviii 27.
nation the Holy of Holies.

XXX.

Since, therefore, we are a portion of the Holy One,
let us do such things as pertain unto holiness,
avoiding evil speaking, foul and impure embraces,
drunkenness, abominable desires, detestable adul-
tery, execrable pride: for God, he saith, resisteth Prov. iii. 34
the proud, but giveth grace unto the humble. Let
us cleave, therefore, to them by whom grace has
been given from God. Let us clothe ourselves
with concord, being humble, temperate, keeping
ourselves far from all whispering and evil speaking,
justified by our deeds, and not by our words. For
he saith, He who saith many things shall, in Job xi. 2, 3
return, hear many things. Doth he that is eloquent
think himself to be just?—doth he that is born of
woman and liveth but for a short time think himself to be blessed? Be not abundant in speech.
Let our praise be in God, and not for ourselves, for
·God hateth the self-praiser. Let the testimony of
right actions be given us from others, even as it
was given to our fathers who were just. Audacity,

self-will, and boldness belong to them who are accursed of God; but moderation, humility, and meekness, to them that are blessed of God.

XXXI.

Let us cleave, therefore, to his blessing, and let us see what are the ways of blessing. Let us consult the records of the things that happened from the beginning. On what account was our father Abraham blessed? Was it not that he wrought righteousness and truth through faith? Isaac, with confidence, knowing the future, willingly became a sacrifice. Jacob, with humility, flying from his brother, went out from his own land and journeyed unto Laban and served as a slave, and there were given unto him the twelve tribes of Israel.

XXXII.

If any one will consider these things severally and one by one, he will recognize the magnificence of the gifts that were given by God. For from Jacob came the priests and all the Levites that serve the altars of God. From him came our Lord Jesus Christ according to the flesh; from him came the kings and rulers and governors of the tribe of Judah; and the remainder of his tribes are of no small glory, since God hath promised, *Gen. xv. 5; xxii. 17; xxvi. 4.* Thy seed shall be as the stars of heaven. All these, therefore, have been glorified and magnified, not through themselves or through their works, or through the righteousness that they have done, but through his will. And we who through his will have been called in Jesus Christ are justified, not by ourselves, or through our wisdom or understanding or godliness, or the works that we have done in holiness of heart, but by faith, by which all men from the beginning have been justified by God Almighty, to whom be glory world without end. Amen.

XXXIII.

What, then, shall we do, brethren? Shall we cease from well-doing, and abandon charity? God forbid that this should happen unto us! but let us rather with diligence and zeal hasten to fulfil every good work. For the Maker and Lord of all things rejoiceth in his works. By his supreme power he founded the heavens, and by his incomprehensible understanding he ordered them. The earth he separated from the water that surrounded it, and fixed it on the firm foundation of his own will. The animals which are there he commanded to be by his ordinance. The sea and the animals that are therein he made beforehand, and shut them in by his own power. Man, the most excellent of all animals, infinite in faculty, he moulded with his holy and faultless hands, in the impress of his likeness. For thus saith God: Let us make man in our own image, and after our own likeness. And God made man. Male and female made he them. Gen. i. 26, 27.

When, therefore, he had finished all things, he praised and blessed them, and said, Be fruitful, and multiply. Let us see, therefore, how all the just have been adorned with good works. Yea, the Lord himself rejoiced when he had adorned himself with his work. Having, therefore, this example, let us come in without shrinking to his will; let us work with all our strength the work of righteousness.

Gen i. 28. (marginal)

XXXIV.

The good workman receiveth boldly the reward of his labour, but the slothful and remiss looketh not his employer in the face. It is therefore right that we should be zealous in well-doing, for from Him are all things; for he telleth us beforehand, Behold the Lord cometh, and his reward is before his face, to give to every one according to his work. He exhorteth us, therefore, with this reward in view, to strive with our whole heart not to be slothful or remiss towards every good work. Let our glorying and our confidence be in him; let us submit ourselves to his will; let us consider the whole multitude of his angels, how they stand by and serve his will. For the scripture saith, Ten thousand times ten thousand and thousands of thousands served him; and they cried, Holy, holy, holy Lord of Sabaoth! all creation is full of his glory. And let us, being gathered together in harmony and a good conscience, cry earnestly, as it were with one mouth, unto him, that we may

(marginal references: Isaiah xl. 10. Prov. xxiv. 12. Rev. xxii. 12. Dan. vii. 10. Isaiah vi. 3.)

XXXV.

Behold, beloved, how blessed and wonderful are the gifts of God—life in immortality, cheerfulness in righteousness, truth in liberty, faith in confidence, temperance in sanctification; and all these things have already come within our cognisance. What therefore are the things that are prepared for them that await his appearing? The Maker and Father of the worlds, the all-holy one, he knoweth how many and how beautiful they are. Let us, therefore, strive to be found in the number of them that await him, that we may partake of the promised gifts. And how will this be, beloved? If our mind be established by faith toward God; if we seek out what is pleasant and acceptable in his sight; if we perform such things as harmonise with his blameless will, and follow in the way of truth, casting from us all unrighteousness and lawlessness, covetousness, strife, malice and fraud, whispering and evil speaking, hatred of God, pride and insolence, vainglory and churlishness. For they who do these things are hateful unto God, and not only they who do them, but also they who have pleasure in them that do them. For the scripture saith:

Ps. i. 16, 23. But unto the sinner God hath said, Why dost thou speak of my ordinances, and takest my covenant in thy mouth: but thou hast hated instruction and hast cast my words behind thee. When thou sawest a thief thou wentest with him, and hast cast in thy portion with the adulterers; thy mouth hath abounded with evil, and thy tongue hath contrived deceit. Thou satest and spakest against thy brother, and hast slandered the son of thy mother. This hast thou done, and I kept silence. Thou thoughtest, O wicked one, that I was like unto thee; but I will convict thee, and set thyself before thee. Consider this, ye who forget God, lest he seize you as a lion, and there be none to save you. The sacrifice of praise shall honour me; and there is the way by which I will show him the salvation of God.

XXXVI.

This is the way, beloved, in which we find our salvation; even Jesus Christ, the high priest of our oblations, the champion and defender of our weakness. Through him we look steadfastly to the heights of heaven; though him we behold, as in a glass, the immaculate and lofty countenance of God the Father; through him the eyes of our heart are opened; through him our foolish and darkened understanding springeth up again to his marvellous light; through him the Lord hath Heb. i. 3. willed us to taste of immortal knowledge, who, being the brightness of his glory, is so far better than the angels, as he hath, by inheritance, obtained

a more excellent name than they. For it is thus
written: Who maketh his angels spirits, his
ministers a flame of fire. But of his Son the
Lord hath thus said: Thou art my son, to-day
have I begotten thee. Ask of me, and I will give
thee the heathen for thine inheritance, the uttermost parts of the world for thy possession. And,
again, he saith unto him: Sit on my right hand
until I make thy enemies thy footstool. Who then
are the enemies? Even the wicked, and they who
resist the will of God.

XXXVII.

Let us, therefore, carry on our warfare with all
earnestness in his holy laws. Let us consider those
who fight under our earthly commanders, how
orderly and obediently and submissively they perform what is commanded them. All are not prefects,
or commanders of thousands, or commanders of
fifties, or such like; but each in his own rank perform-
eth what has been ordered by the king or the commanders. The great cannot exist without the small,
nor the small without the great. There is a certain
mixture in all things, and from thence ariseth their
use. Let us take, for example, our body; the
head is nothing without the feet, nor the feet without the head. The smallest members of the body
are necessary and useful to the whole body, and all
unite and work with harmonious obedience for the
preservation of the whole body.

XXXVIII.

Let, therefore, our whole body be saved in Christ Jesus, and let each be subject to his neighbour, according to the gift which he hath received. Let not the strong man despise the weak, and let the weak pay regard to the strong. Let him that is rich minister to him that is poor. Let him that is poor praise God that he hath given unto him one by whom his want may be supplied. Let the wise show his wisdom, not in words, but in good deeds; let him that is humble not bear witness to himself, but leave another to bear witness to him. Let him that is pure in the flesh boast not of it, knowing that it is another that giveth him the gift of continence. Let us consider, brethren, of what matter we are made, of what sort we are that have come into the world, as it were out of the tomb and darkness. He that made and fashioned us, hath brought us into his world, having prepared beforehand his benefactions, even before we were born. Having, therefore, all these things from him, we ought in all respects to give thanks unto him, to whom be glory world without end. Amen.

XXXIX.

The senseless and unwise, the foolish and unruly, make a mock of us, wishing to exalt themselves in their own imagination. For what can a mortal

do? or what strength hath he that is born of earth?
For it is written, There was no form before my Job iv.
eyes, only I heard a sound and a voice. For 18.
what? shall a man be pure before the Lord? or is
a man blameless from his works? seeing that he
putteth no trust in his servants, and beholdeth somewhat of iniquity in his angels; yea, the heaven is not
pure in his sight. Away, ye who dwell in houses Job xv
of clay, even we who are made of the same clay as Job iv.
our houses. He hath smitten them even as it 21.
were a mote, and in a single day they are no more.
Because they could not help themselves they
perished: he blew among them, and they died,
because they had no wisdom. Call, now, and see Job v
if there be any that I slew; listen to them, if thou
shalt behold any of the holy angels. For anger
destroyeth the fool, and envy putteth him to death;
he is gone out of the way. I have beheld the
foolish casting forth roots, but straightway his habitation was eaten up. Let his sons be far from safety,
let them be mocked at the gates of their inferiors,
and there shall be none to deliver them. For that
which they have prepared the just shall eat, and
they shall not be delivered out of their troubles.

XL.

Since, therefore, these things are manifest unto
us, and since we have looked into the depths of
the divine knowledge, we ought to do everything
in order, whatsoever God hath commanded us to do

the appointed seasons, even to perform the offerings and liturgies. These he hath not commanded to be done at random or in disorder, but at fixed times and seasons. But how and by what means he wisheth them to be fulfilled he himself hath decided by his supreme will; that all things, being done piously, according to his good pleasure, might be acceptable to his will. They, therefore, who at the appointed seasons make their offerings are acceptable and blessed; for they sin not, inasmuch as they obey the laws of God. For to the High Priest were assigned special services, and to the priests a special place hath been appointed; and on the Levites special work hath been imposed. But he that is a layman is bound by the ordinances of laymen.

XLI.

Let each of you, brethren, in his own order, give thanks unto God, continuing in a good conscience, not transgressing the fixed rule of his ministry, with all gravity. Not in every place, brethren, are sacrifices offered continually, either in answer to prayer or concerning sin and neglect, but in Jerusalem only; and even there the offering is not made in every place, but in front of the holy-place at the court of the altar, after that which is offered has been diligently examined by the high priest and the appointed ministers. They, therefore, who do anything contrary to that which is according to his will have for their punishment death. Ye see, brethren, by as much as we have been thought worthy of greater knowledge, by so much the more are we exposed to danger.

XLII.

The Apostles, for our benefit, received the gospel from our Lord Jesus Christ: our Lord Jesus Christ received it from God. Christ, therefore, was sent out from God, and the Apostles from Christ; and both these things were done in good order, according to the will of God. They, therefore, having received the promises, having been fully persuaded by the resurrection of our Lord Jesus Christ, and having been confirmed by the word of God, with the full persuasion of the Holy Spirit, went forth preaching the good tidings that the kingdom of God was at hand. Preaching, therefore, through the countries and cities, they appointed their first fruits to be bishops and deacons over such as should believe, after they had proved them in the Spirit. For the Scripture, in a certain place, saith in this wise: I will establish their bishops in righteousness, and their deacons in faith.

XLIII.

And wherein is it wonderful, if they who, in Christ, were entrusted by God with this work appointed the aforesaid officers? since even the blessed Moses, the faithful servant in all his house, signified in the sacred books all things that were commanded unto him, whom also the prophets have followed, bearing witness to the laws which were appointed by him. For he, when a strife arose concerning the priesthood, and when the tribes contended which of them should be adorned with that glorious name, commanded the twelve chiefs of the tribes to bring to him rods, each inscribed with the name of a tribe; and when he had taken them, he bound them together, and sealed them with the seals of the heads of the tribes, and laid them up on the table of God, in the tabernacle of the testimony. And when he had closed the tabernacle, he sealed the keys, and likewise the rods, and said unto them, Men and brethren, of whatever tribe the rod shall bud, this hath God chosen to be his priest, and to serve him. And when evening was come, he called together all Israel, even six hundred thousand men, and showed unto the heads of the tribes the seals, and opened the tabernacle of the testimony and brought forth the rods, and the rod of Aaron was found not only to have budded, but also bearing fruit. What think ye, beloved? did not Moses know beforehand that this was about to happen? Most assuredly did he know it. But, that there might be no disorder in Israel, he did thus to glorify the name of the true and only God, to whom be glory world without end. Amen.

XLIV.

Our Apostles, too, by the instruction of our Lord Jesus Christ, knew that strife would arise concerning the dignity of a bishop; and on this account, having received perfect foreknowledge, they appointed the above-mentioned bishops and deacons: and then gave a rule of succession, in order that, when they had fallen asleep, other men, who had been approved, might succeed to their ministry. Those who were thus appointed by them, or afterwards by other men of good repute, with the consent of the whole church, who have blamelessly ministered to the flock of Christ with humility, quietly, and without illiberality, and who for a long time have obtained a good report from all, these, we think, have been unjustly deposed from the ministry. For it will be no small sin in us if we depose from their bishoprics those who blamelessly and piously make the offerings. Happy are the presbyters who finished their course before, and died in mature age after they had borne fruit; for they do not fear lest any one should remove them from the place appointed for them. For we see that ye have removed some men of honest conversation from the ministry, which has been blamelessly and honourably performed by them.

XLV.

Ye are contentious, brethren, and are zealous concerning things that pertain not unto salvation. Look diligently into the scriptures, which are the true sayings of the Holy Spirit. Ye know how that nothing unjust or corrupt hath been written in them; for ye will not in them find the just expelled by holy men. The just were persecuted, but it was by the lawless; they were thrown into prison, but it was by the unholy; they were stoned, but it was by sinners; they were slain, but it was by wicked men, even by those who had taken up an unjust envy against them. They, therefore, when they suffered all these things, suffered them with a good report. For what shall we say, brethren? was it by those that feared God that Daniel was cast into the den of lions? Was it by those who practised the magnificent and glorious worship of the Most High that Ananias, Azarias, and Misael, were shut up in the fiery furnace? Let us not suppose that such was the case. Who then were the men who did these things? Abominable men and full of all wickedness were inflamed to such a degree of wrath that they cast into tortures those who, with a holy and a blameless purpose, served God, not knowing that the Most High is a champion and defender of those who with a pure conscience serve his most excellent name, to whom be glory world without end. Amen. But they, abiding steadfastly in their confidence, have inherited honour and glory, and have both been exalted and made beautiful by God, in the memory that is made of them world without end. Amen.

XLVI.

To such examples ought we also to cleave, brethren. For it is written, Cleave unto them that are holy, for they that cleave unto them shall be made holy. And again, in another place he saith, Ps. xv. 26. With the guiltless thou shalt be guiltless, and with the excellent thou shalt be excellent, and with him that is crooked thou shalt be perverse. Let us, therefore, cleave to the guiltless and the just, for they are the elect of God. Why are there strivings, and anger, and division, and war among you? Have ye not one God and one Christ? Is not the spirit of grace, which was poured out upon us, one? is not our calling one in Christ? Why do we tear apart and rend asunder the members of Christ, and make sedition against our body, and come to such a degree of madness that we forget we are members one of another? Remember the words of our Lord Jesus, for he said, Woe unto that man; Matt. xxvi. 24. it were good for him if he had never been born, Matt. xviii 6. rather than that he should cause one of my elect to offend. It were better for him that a millstone Luke xvii. 1, 2. were tied around him, and that he were cast into the sea, rather than that he should cause one of my little ones to offend. This your schism has perverted many; hath cast many into despondency;

many into doubt; all into grief, and, as yet, your sedition remaineth.

XLVII.

Take into your hands the epistle of the blessed apostle Paul. What did he first write unto you in the beginning of his gospel? Of a truth, he warned you spiritually, in a letter, concerning himself, and concerning Cephas and Apollos, because even then there were factions among you; but the faction of that time brought less sin upon you; for ye inclined unto apostles of good repute, and unto a man approved among them. But now consider who they are that have perverted you, and have diminished the glory of your brotherly love, which was known to all men. Disgraceful, brethren, yea, very disgraceful is it, and unworthy of the conduct which is in Christ, that it should be reported that the most firm and ancient church of the Corinthians hath, on account of one or two persons, made sedition against its presbyters. And this report came not only unto us, but also unto the Gentiles, who go not with us. So that ye heap blasphemies on the name of the Lord through your folly, and withal cause danger to yourselves.

XLVIII.

Let us, therefore, remove this as quickly as possible, and let us fall before the feet of our master, and beseech him with tears, that he will have mercy and be reconciled unto us, and restore us again to the grave and pure conversation of brotherly love. For this gate of righteousness is opened unto life, as it is written, Open unto me the gates of righteousness ; I will go in unto them, and give thanks unto the Lord : this is the gate of the Lord ; the righteous shall enter into it. Now, since many gates have been opened, the gate of righteousness is that which is in Christ. Happy are all they that enter therein, and who keep their path straight in holiness and righteousness, quietly performing all their duties. If a man be faithful, if he be mighty to expound knowledge, if he be wise in the interpretation of words, if he be pure in his deeds, by so much the more ought he to be humble, even by as much as he seemeth to be greater, and by so much the more ought he to seek the common advantage of all, and not of himself alone.

Ps. cxviii 19, 20.

XLIX.

Let him that hath the love which is in Christ keep the commandments of Christ. Who can describe sufficiently the bond of the love of God? Who is sufficient to speak as he ought of the excellence of its beauty? The height to which his love leads up is unspeakable. Love joineth us unto God ; love hideth a multitude of sins; love beareth all things ; is long suffering in all things. In love there is nothing illiberal, nothing haughty. Love hath no schism; love maketh not sedition; love doth all things in harmony; in love all the elect of God have been made perfect. Without love nothing is acceptable unto God. In love, our master hath taken us to himself. Through the love that he hath for us, Jesus Christ our Lord hath given himself for us, by the will of God, his flesh for our flesh, his soul for our soul.

L.

Ye see, brethren, how great and wonderful a thing love is, and how there is no describing its perfection. Who is sufficient to be found in it, except those whom God hath deemed worthy? Let us pray, therefore, and ask from his mercy that we may live in love, without human partiality, blameless. All the generations, from Adam even unto this day, are gone by; but they who have been made perfect in love according to the grace of God inhabit the abode of the pious, and shall be made manifest in the visitation of the kingdom of Christ. For it is written, Enter into the secret chambers but a little while, until thy anger and wrath be passed, and I will remember the good day, and will raise you up from your sepulchres. Blessed are we, beloved, if we do the commandments of God in the harmony of love, so that through love our sins may be forgiven us. For it is written, Blessed are they whose iniquities are

Isaiah xxvi. 20.
Ezek. xxxvii. 12.

Ps. xxxii. 1, 2.

LI.

Whatever errors, therefore, we have committed through the assaults of the adversary, let us for these ask pardon; and they who have been leaders of the sedition and division ought to consider the common ground of our hope. For they who have their conversation in fear and love wish that they themselves, rather than their neighbours, should fall into suffering; and would rather that themselves should undergo condemnation, than that the harmony which hath been honourably and justly handed down to us should do so. For it is better that a man should make confession concerning his sins, than that he should harden his heart, even as the heart of them was hardened who made sedition against Moses the servant of God; whose condemnation was manifest, for they went down alive into hell, and death swallowed them up. Pharaoh and his army, and all the leaders of Egypt, their chariots and their riders, through no other cause were sunk in the Red Sea and perished there than through the hardening of their foolish hearts, after that the signs and wonders happened in Egypt through the hand of Moses the servant of God.

Num. xvi 32.

Exod. xiv. 13.

LII.

The Lord of all things, brethren, is in need of naught; neither requireth he anything of any one, except to confess unto him. For the elect David saith, I will confess unto the Lord, and that shall please him more than a young calf that putteth forth horns and hoofs. Let the poor behold and rejoice thereat. And again he saith, Offer unto the Lord the sacrifice of praise: pay thy vows unto the Most High. And call upon me in the day of trouble, and I will deliver thee, and thou shalt glorify me. For the sacrifice unto God is a broken spirit.

LIII.

Ye know, brethren, and know well, the sacred scriptures, and have looked into the oracles of God; call, therefore, these things to remembrance. For, when Moses had gone up into the mount, and had tarried there forty days and forty nights in fasting and humiliation, the Lord said unto him, Moses, Moses, get thee down quickly hence, for thy people, whom thou broughtest out of the land of Egypt, have wrought iniquity. They have gone astray quickly out of the way that I commanded them, and have made unto themselves molten images. And the Lord spake unto him, saying, I have beheld this people, and, lo, it is a stiffnecked people. Let me alone, that I may destroy them,

and I will wipe out their name from under heaven,
and make of thee a nation great and wonderful, and far mightier than they. And Moses
said, Be it far from thee, O Lord. Forgive this Ex xxii. 11
people their sin, and wipe my name out of the
book of the living. Oh, the great love! Oh, the
unsurpassable perfection! The servant is bold
towards the Lord: he asketh remission for the
people, and demandeth that he himself should be
destroyed along with them.

LIV.

Who among you is noble? who is compassionate? who is filled with love? Let him speak in
this wise: If through me sedition and strife arise,
I will depart. I will go away whithersoever ye
will, and I will do that which is commanded by the
church, only let the flock of Christ be at peace
together with the appointed presbyters. He who
doeth this shall gain for himself great glory in the
Lord, and every place shall receive him; for the
earth is the Lord's, and the fulness thereof. These Ps. xxiv. 1
things have they done who are true citizens of
the kingdom of God, and these things will they
yet do.

LV.

But, to bring forward examples from the Gentiles, many kings and leaders, when a time of
pestilence had arisen, being warned by oracles,
gave themselves unto death, that they might deliver

their citizens by their blood. Many went out from their own cities, that there might be no more sedition therein. We know that many among us gave themselves up unto bonds, that they might deliver others. Many have given themselves up unto slavery, and, having received their own price, have therewith fed others. Many women, waxing strong through the grace of God, have performed many manly deeds. The blessed Judith, when the city was shut up, asked of the elders that she should be permitted to go forth into the camp of the aliens. She therefore delivered herself unto danger, and went out through love of her country and of her people, who were besieged. And the Lord delivered Olophernes into the hands of a woman. To no smaller danger did Esther, being perfect in faith, expose herself, that she might deliver the twelve tribes of Israel, who were about to perish. For by fasting and humiliation she besought the Master, who overlooketh all things, the God of Ages, who, seeing the humiliation of her soul, delivered the people for whose sake she put herself in jeopardy.

LVI.

Let us, therefore, pray for those who have fallen into any transgression, that moderation and humility may be given unto them, to the end that they should submit themselves, I do not say unto us, but unto the will of God; for so shall they obtain a fruitful and perfect remembrance and compassion

before God and his saints. Let us accept, brethren,
that discipline at which no one needeth to be
offended. The admonition which we make one
toward another is good and useful exceedingly,
for it joineth us unto the will of God. For thus
speaketh the holy word: The Lord hath chastened me with chastisements, but he hath not
given me over unto death. For whom the Lord
loveth he chasteneth, and scourgeth every son
whom he receiveth. The righteous shall chastise
me in pity and shall rebuke me, but let not the
oil of sinners anoint mine head. And again he
saith: Blessed is the man whom the Lord hath
rebuked; refuse not thou the admonition of the
Almighty, for he maketh thee to grieve, and again
he restoreth thee; he hath smitten, and his hands
have healed thee; six times shall he deliver thee
from calamity, and the seventh time evil shall not
touch thee. In the time of famine he shall deliver
thee from death, in war he shall redeem thee from
the hand of sin. From the scourge of the tongue
shall he hide thee, and thou shalt not be afraid
when evils come upon thee. The unjust and the
sinner shalt thou laugh to scorn; and of the wild
beasts thou shalt not be afraid, for the wild beasts
shall be at peace with thee. Then shalt thou know
that thy house shall be at peace; the habitation of
thy tabernacle shall not fail. Thou shalt know
that thy seed is abundant, thy children like all
the herb of the field. Thou shalt come to thy
tomb like a ripe ear of corn reaped in due season,

like the heap of a threshing-floor that is gathered at its proper time. Ye see, beloved, that there is a protection for them that are chastened by the master, for God chasteneth us because he is good, to the end that we should be admonished by his holy discipline.

LVII.

Do ye, therefore, that have laid the foundation of the sedition submit yourselves to the presbyters, and be chastised to repentance. Bend the knees of your hearts; learn to submit yourselves, laying aside the vain and haughty self-will of your tongues; for it is better that you should be small and approved in the flock of Christ, rather than that, seeming to be superior to others, ye should be cast out of his hope. For thus saith the most excellent wisdom, Behold, I will send upon you the language of my spirit; I will teach you my word. Since I called and ye did not hearken, and prolonged my words, and ye attended not, but made my counsels of none effect, and were not obedient to my reproofs, therefore I will laugh at your destruction, I will exult when desolation cometh upon you; when perturbation hath suddenly come upon you, and ruin is at hand like a whirlwind, when tribulation and oppression cometh upon you. For the time shall come when ye shall call upon me, and I shall not hearken unto you; the wicked shall seek me, and shall not find me. They hated wisdom and chose not the fear of the Lord; they were not willing to attend to my counsels, they mocked at my rebukes. Wherefore they shall eat the fruit of their own way; they shall be filled with their own unrighteousness.

LVIII.

Now, God, who overlooketh all things, who is the master of spirits and Lord of all flesh, who hath chosen our Lord Jesus Christ, and us through him to be a peculiar people, give unto every soul that calleth upon his glorious and holy name, faith, fear, peace, patience, long-suffering, continence, purity, sobriety, to the well-pleasing of his name, through our high priest and protector, Jesus Christ, through whom be ascribed unto him glory and greatness, strength and honour, both now and world without end. Amen.

LIX.

See that ye send back quickly unto us in peace and with joy Claudius Ephebus and Valerius Bito, who were sent unto you from us, that they may the more quickly bring us news of your peace and order, which we pray for and desire, so that we may the sooner have joy concerning your good order.

The grace of our Lord Jesus Christ be with you, and with all who everywhere are called of God through him, to whom be glory, honour, might, majesty, and eternal dominion, world without end. Amen.

The Second Epistle of S. Clement.

I.

BRETHREN, we ought so to think of our Lord Jesus Christ as of God, as of the judge of quick and dead, and we ought not to think meanly concerning our salvation; for if we think meanly concerning it, we expect that we shall receive mean things; and if we listen to it as though it were a small thing, we are not knowing from whence we are called, nor by whom, nor unto what place, nor what great things Jesus Christ hath endured to suffer on our behalf. What recompense, therefore, shall we give unto him, or what fruit worthy of that which he hath given unto us? How many things that help unto holiness hath he given unto us? For he hath given us the light, he hath addressed us as a father doth his son, he hath saved us when we were ready to perish. What praise, therefore, shall we give unto him, or what recompense of reward for the things that we have received; for we were maimed in our understanding, worshipping stocks and stones, and gold and silver

and iron, the work of men, and our whole life was
nothing but death. We, therefore, who were surrounded with darkness, and who had our sight filled
with such gloom, have recovered our sight, having,
according to his will, laid aside the cloud that was
around us. For he hath had compassion upon us,
and, pitying us, hath saved us, having beheld in us
much wandering and destruction, when we had no
hope of salvation except from him. For he hath
called us when as yet we were not, and hath willed
us to be when we were nothing.

II.

Rejoice, thou barren that bearest not; break forth
and shout, thou that travailest not, for the desolate
hath many more children than she that hath an
husband. In that he said, Rejoice, thou barren that
bearest not, he hath spoken of us, for our church was
barren before that children were given unto her.
But in that he said, Shout, thou that travailest not,
he meaneth that we should offer up prayer to God
with humility, that we faint not like women in
travail. But in that he said, The children of the
desolate are many more than they of her that hath
an husband, he meaneth that our people seemed
to be deserted of God, and now, after that we have
believed, we have become more in number than
they which seemed to have God. And another
Scripture saith, I came not to call the righteous but
sinners. This he saith because it behoveth him to

save them that are perishing. For this is great and wonderful, not to establish the things that are standing, but the things that are falling; thus Christ willed to save the things that were perishing, and he saved many, having come and called us who were perishing.

III.

Since, therefore, he hath showed such compassion unto us; chiefly first, in that he hath caused that we who live should not sacrifice unto gods that are dead, neither worship them, but know through him the father of truth, wherein doth this knowledge consist, except in not denying him through whom we know him? For he himself saith, Whosoever confesseth me before men, him will I confess before my father. This, therefore, is our reward if we confess him through whom we have been saved. But whereby shall we confess him? Even by doing what he commandeth, and not disobeying his commandments, and honouring him not only with our lips but with our whole heart and whole understanding. For he saith in Esaias, This people honoureth me with their lips, but their heart is far from me.

Matt x 32.

Isaiah xxix. 13.

IV.

Let us not, therefore, only call him Lord, for that will not save us. For he saith, It is not every one that sayeth unto me, Lord, Lord! that shall be saved, but he that doeth righteousness. Where-

Matt. vii. 21.

fore, brethren, let us confess him in our deeds, by loving one another, by not committing adultery, and not speaking ill of each other, neither being envious, but by being continent, compassionate, kind. We ought also to sympathize one with another, and to abstain from covetousness; it is by these works that we acknowledge God, and not by the contrary; and we ought not to fear men but rather God. Wherefore, if we do these things, the Lord hath said, If ye are gathered together with me in my bosom and do not my commandments I will cast you from me, and I will say unto you, Depart from me; I know you not whence ye are, ye workers of iniquity.

V.

Wherefore, brethren, leaving our sojourning in this world, let us do the will of him who called us, and let us not fear to depart from this world. For the Lord saith, Ye shall be as lambs in the midst of wolves. But Peter answered and saith unto him, What then if the wolves rend the sheep? Jesus saith unto Peter, Let not the lambs after that they are dead fear the wolves; and do not ye fear them that kill you but can do nothing more unto you, but fear him who after ye are dead hath authority over body and soul, even to cast them into the hell fire. And ye know, brethren, that the sojourning of our flesh in this world is but short and for a little while, but the promise of Christ is great and wonderful, even the rest of the kingdom which is to come and of eternal life. What, therefore, shall we do that we may attain unto them, except to lead a holy and just conversation, and to deem the things of this world to be alien unto us? for while we desire to acquire these things we fall from the right way.

VI.

For the Lord saith, No servant can serve two masters. If, therefore, we wish to serve both God and Mammon, it is inexpedient for us; for what advantage is it if a man gain the whole world, but lose his soul? Now this life and the life to come are two enemies. This life preacheth adultery, corruption, covetousness, and deceit; but the life that is to come renounceth these things. We cannot, therefore, be friends to both; it behoveth us then to renounce the one and to use the other. Let us consider, therefore, that it is better to hate the things that are here, as being small and short-lived and corruptible, but to love the things that are there, as being good and incorruptible. If, therefore, we do the will of Christ, we shall find rest; but if not, nothing will deliver us from eternal punishment, if we obey not his commandments. For the Scripture saith in Ezekiel, If Noah, and Job, and Daniel rise up, they shall not deliver their children in the captivity. If, therefore, such righteous men as these cannot by their righteousness deliver their children, with what confidence shall we, if we keep not our baptism pure and undefiled, come unto the kingdom of God? or who shall be our advocate unless we be found having the works that are holy and just?

VII.

Wherefore, my brethren, let us strive, knowing that the contest is at hand. We know, too, that many put in for corruptible contests, but all are not crowned, but they only who have laboured much and fought a good fight. Let us, therefore, so fight that we may all be crowned. Let us run in the straight course, in the incorruptible contest ; and let us be many that put into it, and let us contend so that we may be crowned. And if we cannot all be crowned, let us at least come near to the crown. It behoveth us to know that he who contendeth in a corruptible contest, if he be found acting unfairly is flogged, and taken away, and cast out of the course. What think ye? what shall he suffer that acteth unfairly in an incorruptible contest? For of them who have not kept their seal he saith, Their worm shall die not, and their fire shall not be quenched, and they shall be for a spectacle to all flesh.

VIII.

While, therefore, we are upon the earth, let us repent. For we are as clay in the hands of the workman. In like manner as the potter, if while he be making a vessel, it turn amiss or be crushed in his hands, can mould it again, but if he have once cast it into the fiery furnace can no longer amend it; so let us, so long as we are in this world repent with all our hearts of the wickedness that we have committed in the flesh, that we may be saved of the Lord while as yet we have time for repentance. For after that we are departed out of this world, we are no longer able to confess or repent. Wherefore, brethren, if we have done the will of the Father, and preserved our flesh pure, and kept the commandments of the Lord, we shall receive eternal life. For the Lord saith in the Gospel, If ye have not kept that which is little, who shall give you that which is great? for I say unto you he that is faithful in that which is least is faithful also in much. Doth he not, therefore, say this, Keep your flesh pure and your seal unspotted, that ye may inherit eternal life?

IX.

And let not any one of you say that this our flesh is not judged nor raised again. Consider this: in what were ye saved, in what did ye recover your sight, if not in the flesh? We ought, therefore, to guard our flesh as the temple of God; for in the same manner as ye were called in the flesh, in the flesh also shall ye come. There is one Christ our Lord who saved us, who being at the first spirit, was made flesh, and thus called us. Let us, therefore, love one another, that we may all come to the kingdom of God. While we have opportunity to be healed, let us give ourselves up unto God who healeth, giving a recompense unto him. And what is this? repentance from a sincere heart. For he foreknoweth all things, and knoweth the things that are in our hearts. Let us, therefore, give him praise, not from the mouth alone, but also from the heart, that he may receive us as sons. For of a truth the Lord hath said, My brethren are they who do the will of my Father.

X.

Wherefore, my brethren, let us do the will of the Father who hath called us, that we may live; and let us the rather pursue virtue, and abandon vice which leadeth us into sins. and let us fly ungodliness lest evil seize us; for if we are zealous to do good peace shall pursue us. For this cause it is not possible that a man should find peace. For they introduce the fear of men, choosing rather the present enjoyment that is here than the future promise. For they are ignorant how great a torment the present enjoyment bringeth, and what delight hath the future promise. And if they alone did these things it were endurable; but now they continue to instruct in evil innocent souls, not knowing that they will have a twofold condemnation—both themselves and they that hearken to them.

XI.

Let us, therefore, serve God with a pure heart, and we shall be righteous; but if we serve him not, because we believe not the promises of God, we shall be wretched. For the prophetic word saith, Wretched are the double-minded who doubt in their hearts, and say, We have heard these things even in the time of our fathers, but we have seen none of them, though we expect them from day to day. Ye fools, compare yourselves unto a tree; take for an example the vine. In the first place it sheddeth its leaves, then there cometh a shoot, after that the unripe grape, then the mature cluster. In like manner my people hath in time past had disorder and trouble, but afterward it shall receive the things that are good. Wherefore, my brethren, let us not be double-minded, but let us abide in hope, that we may obtain our reward. Faithful is he that hath promised that he will give unto each the recompense of his works. If, therefore, we do righteousness before God, we shall enter into his kingdom, and receive the promises which ear hath not heard nor eye seen, neither have entered into the heart of man.

XII.

Let us, therefore, in love and righteousness expect every hour the kingdom of God, since we know not the day of the appearing of God. For the Lord himself, when he was asked by a certain man when his kingdom should come, replied, When two shall be one, and that which is without as that which is within, and the male with the female neither male nor female. Now two are one when we speak the truth one to another, and there is, without hypocrisy, one soul in two bodies. And by that which is without being as that which is within, he meaneth this: He calleth the soul that which is within, and the body that which is without; in like manner, therefore, as thy body is visible, let thy soul be made manifest by good deeds. And by the male with the female neither male nor female, he meaneth this—

The remainder of the epistle is lost, but a conclusion to the chapter may be supplied from Clement of Alexandria. Strom. iii. 13, 553.

He calleth, as it were, in a riddle, our anger the male, our lust the female. But when lust and anger have done their work, then follow repentance and shame. When, therefore, a man gratifieth neither his lust nor his anger, both which things, having grown up from custom and evil nurture, overshadow and darken the reason, but having dispersed the mist that ariseth from them, being full of the shame that cometh of repentance, shall unite his soul and spirit in obedience to reason, then is it, as Paul saith, There is among you neither male nor female.

Fragment I.—Let it not trouble your hearts that we see the unjust rich, and the servants of God in straits. For none of the just receiveth a speedy recompense, but waiteth for it. For if God gave straightway the reward of the righteous, we should practise gain and not godliness. For we should seem to be just not from godliness, but as following after gain. Johan. Damascenus. S. Parall. i. 783.

Fragment II.—He who is able to perceive the things that are present understandeth that those things which some consider delightful are not alien and far removed from those that are hateful. Yea, of a truth, wealth hath often afflicted more than poverty, and health caused more pain than disease. And generally the compassing of what is pleasant and desired becometh in the end the cause and matter of what is painful and to be avoided. Johan. Damascenus, ii. 987.

Fragment III.—The love of man toward God is sufficient for salvation. For it is the part of gratitude to preserve love toward him who is the cause of our being, by which love we are brought safe to a second life that groweth not old.

Fragment IV.—God did tempt Abraham, not because he was ignorant what manner of man he was, but that he might show him to them that came afterward, and might not conceal such a man, and that he might stir up others to the imitation of his faith and patience, and might persuade them to neglect even their love toward their children in comparison of the fulfilment of the command of God. For which cause he provided that there should be a written history of him. Johan. Damascenus, i. 49, 752.

Fragment V.—It is not just that when the giver is neglected the gifts should remain with those that are ungrateful. S. Maximus, serm. viii.

Fragment VI.—There is a difference between truth and custom. Truth is discovered by being sought for with sincerity. But whatever kind of habit may have been acquired, whether it be true or false, is kept up by its own strength, without being submitted to any examination. For each delights to remain in the habits to which he has been accustomed from a child. Bodleian MSS. 143. Barocc.

Fragment VII.—God liveth, and the Lord Jesus Christ, and the Holy Spirit. Basil. lib. de Spiritu Sancto, iii. 61.

Fragment VIII.—That we who were nothing before we were made may come into being at his will, and enjoy the things that were made for our sakes. For this cause are we men, and have understanding and reason, having received them from him. Leontius (Mai. Script. Vet. Nov. Coll. vii. 84).

The Epistle of S. Barnabas.

The Epistle of S. Barnabas.

I.

HAIL, my sons and daughters, in the name of our Lord Jesus Christ, who hath loved us in peace.

I rejoice exceedingly and beyond measure at your happy and glorious spirit, since the ordinances of God are great and rich towards you; for so have ye received the engrafted grace of the spiritual gift. Wherefore, I congratulate myself the more, hoping to be saved, because I see of a truth the spirit poured out upon you from the rich Lord of love. So greatly hath your longed-for appearance stricken me with amazement. Being persuaded, therefore, of this, and knowing in myself that since I spake among you the Lord hath helped me in many things in the way of righteousness, I am altogether compelled to love you even beyond my own soul, because great faith and love dwelleth in you in the hope of his life. Considering also this, that if I take

care to communicate to you a part of that which
I have received, it shall turn to my reward to
have assisted such spirits as ye are, I gave diligence
to write unto you in few words, in order that
together with your faith, ye might have your knowledge perfect also. For there are three doctrines
ordained of the Lord: the hope of life, the begin-
ing, and the end. For the master hath made known
unto us by the prophets the things which are past,
and the things which are at hand, and hath given
us the first fruits of the knowledge of the things that
are to come. Since, therefore, we see all these
things severally working as he has spoken, we
ought the more fully and loftily to approach to his
altar; but I, not as a master, but as one of yourselves, will show to you a few things, by means of
which ye may even in this present rejoice.

II.

Since, therefore, the days are evil, and the adversary hath the authority, we ought to take heed
to ourselves and seek out the ordinances of the
Lord. For the helpers of our faith are fear and
patience, and they that fight on our side are long-
suffering and continence. While these, therefore,
remain pure in things relating to the Lord, wisdom
and understanding, science and knowledge, rejoice
together with them. For God hath made known
unto us through all the prophets, that he desireth
neither sacrifices nor whole burnt offerings, nor

oblations; for he saith in a certain place, To what
purpose is the multitude of your sacrifices? saith
the Lord. I am full of the whole burnt offerings of
rams; I desire not the fat of lambs, nor the blood
of bulls and goats, nor need ye come to be seen of
me. For who hath required these things at your
hands? Ye shall not add thereto to tread my court.
If ye bring a cake of fine wheat, it is vain; incense
is an abomination unto me; your new moons and
sabbaths I cannot endure; your fastings and
holidays and feasts my soul hateth. These things,
therefore, he hath made of none effect, that the
new law of our Lord Jesus Christ, being free from
the yoke of necessity, might have an offering not
made with hands. Again, he saith unto them, Did
I command your fathers, when ye came out of the
land of Egypt, offer unto me whole burnt offerings
and sacrifices?—did I not rather command them
this?—Let each of you bear no malice against his
neighbour in his heart, and love not a false oath. We
ought to perceive, since we are not void of understanding, the meaning of the goodness of God our
father, because he telleth us, wishing to seek us who
are wandering even as sheep, how we ought to approach him. He therefore speaketh unto us in this
wise: The sacrifice unto God is a broken heart; a
smell of sweet savour unto the Lord is a heart that
glorifieth him that made it. We ought, therefore,
brethren, to examine accurately concerning our salvation, lest the evil one, making an entrance among
us, should draw us away from our life.

III.

Therefore, he saith again, concerning these things unto them, Why fast ye unto me, saith the Lord, so that your voice is heard to-day in its crying? This is not the fast that I have chosen, saith the Lord, for a man to humiliate his soul; nor if ye bend your neck as a ring, and put under you sackcloth and ashes—not even then will ye call it an acceptable fast. But unto us he saith, Behold the fast which I have chosen, saith the Lord, not that a man should humiliate his soul, but that he should loose every bond of unrighteousness, and untie the knots of the compacts of violence; set at liberty them that are bruised, and break every agreement of unrighteousness; break thy bread with the hungry, and if thou seest the naked, clothe him; bring them that are houseless into thy dwelling, and if thou seest a man that is lowly, despise him not, and turn not away from those of thy family; then shall thy light break forth early, and thy garments shall spring up quickly, and justice shall go before thee, and the glory of the Lord shall surround thee; then shalt thou cry, and the Lord shall hearken unto thee; while thou art yet speaking he shall say, Lo, I am here. If thou put away from thee the chain and the false oath, and the word of murmuring, and givest thy bread unto the hungry with all thine heart, and hast compassion upon the soul that is lowly. The long-suffering God therefore having seen before-

IV.

It behoveth, therefore, that we, searching much concerning the things that are at hand, should seek out the things that are able to save us. Let us fly, therefore, utterly from all the work of unrighteousness, and let us hate the error of the time that now is, that we may be loved in that which is to come. Let us not give liberty unto our soul that it should have leave to run with sinners and evil men, neither let us be made like unto them. The tribulation being made perfect is at hand, concerning which it is written, as Enoch saith, For to this purpose the Lord hath cut short the times and the days, that his beloved might make haste and come into his inheritance. The prophet also speaketh in this wise: Ten kingdoms shall reign upon the earth; and there shall rise up after them a little king who shall humble three of the kings under one. And in like manner Daniel speaketh concerning him: And I saw the fourth beast, evil and strong and harder than all the beasts of the earth; and I saw how there grew up from him ten horns, and from among them a little horn, growing up beside, and how it humbled under one three of the great horns. Ye ought, therefore, to understand. And moreover I ask this of you, as being one among you, loving you specially and altogether, even above my own soul, that ye should take heed unto yourselves, and not be like unto certain men, by adding to your sins and saying that their covenant is also ours. Ours, indeed, it is; but they have lost it for ever, in this wise, after that Moses had already received it. For the Scripture saith, And Moses was in the mount fasting forty days and nights, and he received the covenant from the Lord; even tables of stone written with the finger of the hand of the Lord. But when they turned unto idols they lost it. For the Lord saith thus unto Moses, Moses, get thee down quickly, for thy people, whom thou broughtest out of the land of Egypt, have done unlawfully. And Moses understood, and cast the two tables from his hands, and the covenant that was on them was broken; to the end that that of the beloved Jesus might be sealed in our hearts in the hope of his faith. Now, though I wished to write many things unto you, not as a master, but even as suiteth one that loveth you, not to fall short of the things that we have, I have been zealous to write unto you as though I were the offscouring of you. Let us, therefore, give heed unto the last days; for the whole time of our faith will profit us nothing unless now, in the season of iniquity and among the stumbling-blocks that are coming, we resist as becometh the sons of God, that the evil one may not have entrance unawares. Let us fly all vanity and hate perfectly the deeds of the evil way. Do not, entering into your own houses, dwell alone, as though ye were already justified, but coming together, enquire one with another concerning the common advantage. For the Scripture saith, Woe unto them that are wise in their own conceit and learned in their own eyes. Let us be spiritual: let us be a perfect temple unto God. So far as in you lieth, let us practise the fear of God, and strive to keep his commandments, that we may be glad in his ordinances. The Lord shall judge the world without respect of persons; each shall receive according as he hath done; if he be good, righteousness shall go before him, but if he be evil, the reward of wickedness shall be before him. Let us give heed that we do not, as being already elect, take rest, and sleep in our sins, lest the ruler of wickedness, getting the mastery over us, thrust us from the kingdom of the Lord. And, moreover, my brethren, consider this. When ye see that after so many signs and wonders that have happened in Israel, even then they have been abandoned, let us take heed lest, as it is written, many of us be called but few chosen.

V.

For on this account the Lord endured to give his flesh unto corruption, that we might be sanctified by the remission of sins, which is by the sprinkling of his blood. For there are written concerning him certain things that pertain unto Israel, and certain other that pertain unto us. For he speaketh thus, He was wounded for our iniquities, and vexed for our sins; by his stripes we are healed. He was led as a sheep unto the slaughter, and like a dumb lamb before him that sheareth it. We ought, therefore, to give especial thanks unto the Lord because he hath made known unto us the things that are past, and hath made us wise with regard to those that are at hand, neither are we without understanding as regards the future. For the Scripture saith, Not unjustly is the net stretched for the birds. Meaning thereby that a man will perish justly who, having a knowledge of the path of righteousness, shutteth himself up into the way of darkness. Consider this too, my brethren; if the Lord endured to suffer for our souls, though he were the Lord of the whole world, to whom God said from the foundation of the world, Let us make man according to our image and according to our likeness, how then did he endure to suffer at the hands of men? Learn ye! The prophets having received the grace from him prophesied with regard to him. But he, that he might make death of none effect and bring to light the resurrection from the dead, because it behoved him to be made manifest in the flesh, endured it, that he might give unto our fathers the promise, and by preparing for himself a new people, might show while upon earth that he will raise the dead and himself execute judgment. Yea, further; though he taught Israel and did so many signs and wonders among them, yet they loved him not.

But when he chose out his own apostles, who were about to preach his Gospel, they were men unrighteous beyond all sin, that he might show that he came not to call the righteous but sinners to repentance. Then he made himself manifest that he was the Son of God. For if he had not come in the flesh how could men have looked upon him and be saved, since they cannot endure to look at the rays of the sun which must one day perish, and which is the work of his hands? For this purpose did the Son of God come in the flesh, that he might sum up and finish the sin of them who persecuted his prophets unto death; therefore he endured even unto this. For God saith that the smiting of his flesh it was from them. When they shall smite their shepherd, then shall the sheep of the flock be scattered. But he himself wished thus to suffer, for it was necessary that he should suffer upon the cross; for he who prophesieth about him saith, Spare my soul from the sword, and drive nails into my flesh, for the synagogues of evil men have risen against me. And again he saith, Behold, I have given my back unto the scourging and my cheeks unto buffetings; my face also have I set as a hard rock.

VI.

When, therefore, he made the commandment what sayeth he? Who is he that disputeth with me? let him resist me; or who is he that contendeth with me? let him draw nigh unto the Son of the

Lord. Woe unto you, for you shall all wax old as a garment, and the moth shall devour you. And again the prophet saith, Since he hath been placed, as a strong stone, for crushing; behold I will place on the foundation of Zion a stone precious, elect, a chief corner stone of great price. And then what saith he? And he that believeth in him shall live for ever. Is then our hope in a stone? God forbid. But it is said because the Lord hath made strong his flesh, for he saith, And he made me as it were a hard rock. And again, The stone which the builders rejected hath become the head of the corner. And again he saith, This is the day great and wonderful which the Lord hath made. I write unto you the more simply that ye may understand. I am the off-scouring of your love. What then saith the prophet again? The synagogue of the wicked came around me; they surrounded me as bees do an honey-comb, and over my garment they cast lots. Since, therefore, he was about to be made manifest and to suffer in the flesh, his suffering was showed beforehand. For the prophet saith unto Israel, Woe unto their soul, for they have counselled an evil counsel among themselves, saying, let us bind the righteous because he is inconvenient unto us. And what saith the other prophet even Moses unto them? Behold, thus saith the Lord God: Enter into the good land which the Lord sware unto Abraham and Isaac and Jacob, and inherit it, even a land flowing with milk and honey. What saith the knowledge?

Learn ye. Hope, it saith, upon Jesus, who is about to be manifested unto you in the flesh. For man is but earth which suffers. For, from the face of the ground was made the moulding of Adam. What then meaneth he when he saith, Into the good land which floweth with milk and honey? Blessed be the Lord, brethren, who hath put into you wisdom and knowledge of his secret things. For the prophet speaketh a parable from the Lord. Who shall understand, except he that is wise and skilful and that loveth his Lord? Since, therefore, having renewed us by the remission of our sins, he hath made us of a new character, he willeth that we should have the souls of children, inasmuch as it is indeed he who hath formed us anew. For the Scripture saith concerning us, that he saith unto the Son, Let us make man after our own image and according to our likeness; and let them rule over the beasts of the earth, and the fowls of heaven, and the fishes of the sea. And the Lord said when he saw how excellent our form was, Increase and multiply and replenish the earth. These things he saith unto the Son. Again I will show unto thee how the Lord speaketh unto us. He hath fashioned us anew in these last days. The Lord saith, Behold I make the last even as the first. For to this purpose did the prophet preach. Enter ye into the land flowing with milk and honey and have dominion over it. Behold now we have been formed again, even as he saith again in another prophet. Behold, saith the Lord, I will take out

Gen. i. 26.

Gen. i. 28.

Exod. xxxiii. 3.

Ezek. xi. 19. xxxvi. 26.

from these, that is out of those whom the spirit of the Lord foresaw, the hearts of stone, and will put into them hearts of flesh, because he himself was about to be manifested in the flesh and to dwell among us. For the habitation of our heart is a temple holy unto the Lord. For the Lord saith again, Whereby shall I appear before the Lord my God and be glorified? He saith too, I will give thanks unto thee in the assembly, in the midst of my brethren; I will sing unto thee in the midst of the assembly of the saints. We are, therefore, those whom he brought into the good land. What then meaneth the milk and honey? It is because a child is kept alive, first with honey, afterwards with milk. So we, too, being quickened by faith in his promise and by his word, shall live and rule over the earth. And we said above, And let them increase and multiply and rule over the fish. Who then is he who is able to rule over the beasts, the fish, and fowls of heaven? For we ought to perceive that to rule belongeth to authority, so that a man by giving commands may exercise lordship. If, therefore, this doth not take place now, he hath told us when it will; even when we ourselves have been made perfect, so that we become heirs of the covenant of the Lord.

VII.

Ye perceive, therefore, beloved children, that our good Lord hath manifested unto us all things beforehand, to the end that we should know

whom we ought to praise, returning thanks for
all things. If, therefore, the Son of God, being
he who is the Lord and who is about to judge the
quick and the dead, suffered, to the end that his
stripes might make us live, let us believe that the
Son of God could not suffer except on our account.
But being crucified, he drank vinegar and gall.
How, then, did the priests of the temple signify
concerning this? Now, the commandment is written
in this wise: Whosoever shall not fast on the fast, Lev. xxiii. 29.
he shall die the death, the Lord hath commanded
it. Since he also was about to offer the vessel
that contained his spirit as a sacrifice, in order
that the type might be fulfilled which was given
by the offering of Isaac at the altar. What,
therefore, saith he in the book of the prophet?
And let them eat of the goat which is offered on
the fast for the sins of all. Attend ye diligently
thereto. And let the priests alone eat of the un-
washed entrails with vinegar. With what signification? Because ye will one day give me to drink
of vinegar and gall, when I am about to offer up
my flesh for my new people. Eat ye it alone,
while the people fast and lament in sackcloth and
ashes. He commanded this in order that he might
show that he must needs suffer at their hands.
How, then, did he give his commands? Attend
ye. Take ye two goats, fair and like each other, Lev. xvi. 7.
and offer them up. And let the priest take one
of them as a whole burnt offering for sin. But
what shall they do with the other? Let the other,

he saith, be accursed. Now attend ye, how the type of Jesus is made manifest. And do ye all spit upon it and pierce it, and put scarlet wool around its head, and so let it be cast out into the wilderness. And when this hath been done, he who beareth the goat leadeth it out into the wilderness, and taketh away the wool and placeth it upon a bush, which is called rachel, the shoots of which we are accustomed to eat when we find them in the fields. Thus the fruit of the rachel only is sweet. What, therefore, meaneth this? Attend ye. One is brought to the altar, the other is accursed, and the accursed one is crowned, because they shall see him in that day, who had the scarlet robe about his flesh, and they shall say, Is not this he whom once we set at naught and crucified, and spat upon and pierced? Truly this was he who at that time said that he was the Son of God. How then was he like unto that goat? In this respect were the goats like him: they were fair and equal, so that when they saw him coming they were astonished at the likeness to the goat. Therefore, behold here the type of Jesus, who was about to suffer. And what meaneth the wool placed in the midst of thorns? It is a type of Jesus, which hath been placed in the church. For he who wisheth to take the scarlet wool must suffer many things, because the thorn is terrible, and must after tribulation gain possession of it. So he saith, They who wish to see me and to take hold of my kingdom must through trouble and suffering receive me.

VIII.

And what type, think ye, was the commandment unto Israel, that the men in whom sin had been accomplished should offer a heifer, and after they had slaughtered it should burn it, and that children should then take the ashes and cast them into vessels, and place scarlet wool and hyssop around a stick—behold, again, the type of the cross and the scarlet wool—and so the boys should sprinkle the people one by one, that they might be purged from their sins? Behold, therefore, in what way he speaketh unto you with simplicity. The heifer signifieth Jesus: they who offer it are the sinful men who brought him unto the slaughter. But now the men are no longer before us, no longer doth the glory belong to sinners. The boys who sprinkled are they who brought us the good news of the forgiveness of sins and purification of heart, to whom he hath given the authority of the gospel for the purpose of preaching, being twelve in number, for a testimony unto the tribes, for twelve were the tribes of Israel. And why, then, these boys who sprinkle? For a testimony unto Abraham, Isaac, and Jacob, because these are great before God. And what signifieth the wool upon the stick? Because the kingdom of Jesus is upon the cross, and because they who hope upon him shall live for ever. And why are there at the same time the wool and the hyssop? Because in his kingdom the days in which we shall be saved shall be evil and filthy, because he that grieveth his flesh is healed through the purifying of the hyssop. And these things having happened on this account are manifest unto us, but obscure unto them, because they hearkened not unto the voice of the Lord.

IX.

He saith also again concerning our ears how he hath circumcised our heart. The Lord saith in the prophet, They have hearkened unto me with the hearing of their ears; and again, he saith, They that are afar off shall hear with their ears; they shall know what I have done; and be ye circumcised, saith the Lord, in your heart; and again, Hear, O Israel, for thus saith the Lord thy God; and again the spirit of the Lord prophesied, Who is he that wisheth to live for ever? let him hearken unto the voice of my son. And again he saith, Hear, O heaven, and give ear, O earth, for the Lord hath spoken these things for a testimony. And again he saith, Hearken unto the voice of the Lord, ye rulers of this people. And again he saith, Hearken ye children unto the voice of one crying in the wilderness. To this end, therefore, hath he circumcised our hearing, that when we hear his word, we should believe; for the circumcision in which they trust is done away with. For he hath said that circumcision is not that which was made in the flesh; but they have transgressed, for an evil angel hath

deluded them. He saith unto them, These things
saith the Lord your God,—here I find a new
commandment—Sow not among thorns, but be ye
circumcised unto your Lord. And what saith he?
Circumcise the hardness of your hearts, and harden
not your neck. And again, Behold, saith the Lord,
all the Gentiles are uncircumcised in their foreskin,
but this people is uncircumcised in their hearts.
But he will say, Of a truth the people have been
circumcised for a seal unto them ; but so, also, hath
every Syrian and Arabian, and all the priests of
idols. Do they also belong to the covenant? But
the Egyptian also are in circumcision. Learn, therefore, children of love, richly concerning all things,
that Abraham, who first gave circumcision, circumcised, looking forward in the spirit unto Jesus,
having received the doctrines of the three letters.
For he saith, And Abraham circumcised out of his
household eighteen and three hundred. What,
then, was the knowledge that was given unto this
man? Behold, he mentioned the eighteen first, and
then, having made an interval, he mentioneth the
three hundred. In the eighteen, IH, you have
Jesus ; and because the cross in the letter T was
about to convey the grace of redemption, he
mentioneth also the three hundred. Therefore, he
showeth Jesus in the two letters, IH, and the cross
in the one, T. He knoweth this who hath
placed the engrafted gift of his teaching in us. No
one hath had from me a more true account than
this ; but I know that ye are worthy.

X.

But in that Moses said, Thou shalt not eat the swine, nor the eagle, nor the hawk, nor the crow, nor any fish that hath not scales in itself, he had in his mind these doctrines. For in the end he saith unto them in Deuteronomy, And I will arrange before this people my ordinances. The commandment of God is not, therefore, that they should not eat; but Moses spake in a spiritual sense. He spake of the swine with this meaning: Thou shalt not cleave, he meaneth, unto men of this sort, who are like unto swine, for when they become wanton they forget their Lord, but when they are in want they think upon the Lord; even as the swine when it eateth knoweth not its lord, but when it is hungry it crieth, and when it hath received it is again silent. Nor shalt thou eat of the eagle, nor of the hawk, nor of the kite, nor of the crow. Thou shalt not, he meaneth, cleave to, nor be like to men of this sort, who know not how to provide sustenance for themselves by labour and sweat, but in their iniquity seize the property of others, and, as though they walked in innocence, watch and observe whom they shall plunder, through their covetousness; even as these birds alone provide not sustenance for themselves by means of toil, but, sitting idle, seek out how they may eat the flesh of others, being destructive by reason of their wickedness. And thou shalt not eat, he saith, of the lamprey, or the

polypus, or the cuttle-fish. Thou shalt not, he
meaneth, cleave to or become like unto men
of this sort, who are impious unto the end, and
have been already condemned to death, even
as these accursed fish alone swim in the depth,
not floating as the others do, but dwelling in
the earth below the depth of the sea. Thus,
he saith, Thou shalt not eat the hare, meaning
thou shalt not indulge in unnatural lusts; nor
shalt thou eat the hyæna, meaning thou shalt n t
be an adulterer; nor shalt thou eat the weazel,
meaning thou shalt not do uncleanness with thy
mouth concerning food; therefore Moses spake
in the spirit these three doctrines. But they,
according to the lusts of their flesh, received them
as being about meat. And David receiveth knowledge concerning the same three doctrines, and
saith in like manner, Blessed is the man who hath P.
not walked in the counsel of the ungodly, even as
the fish walk in darkness into the depths of the sea,
and hath not stood in the way of sinners, even as
they who pretend to fear the Lord sin as doth the
swine, and hath not sat in the seat of the destroyers,
even as the birds that sit for prey. Ye have also in
the end a commandment concerning food; but
Moses said, Eat ye everything that is cloven-footed Lev
and that cheweth the cud. What meaneth he? He
that taketh food knoweth him that feedeth him,
and, resting upon him, seemeth to be glad. He
therefore saith well, having regard to the commandment. What then meaneth he? Cleave ye unto

them that fear the Lord, who walk in his commandments, which they have received in their hearts; unto them that speak of the ordinances of the Lord, and observe them, unto them who know that the practice of them is a work of gladness, and who ruminate on the word of the Lord. But what meaneth that which cleaveth the hoof? It meaneth that the just walketh even in this world, and expecteth the holy life. See how well Moses hath laid down the law; but how was it possible for them to perceive or understand these things? But we, having rightly understood the commandments, speak them even as the Lord hath willed. On this account hath he circumcised our ears and hearts, that we should understand these things.

XI.

Let us inquire, therefore, if the Lord cared to show us beforehand concerning the water and concerning the cross. Concerning the water it is written, with respect to Israel, how that they will not receive the baptism that bringeth remission of sins, but will establish one for themselves. The prophet therefore speaketh in this wise, Be astonished, O heaven! and let the earth shudder still more at this, because this people hath done two great and evil things: they have abandoned me who am the fountain of life, and have dug for themselves broken cisterns. Is my holy mountain of Zion a deserted rock? ye shall be as the unfledged young of a bird when the nest has been taken away. And again the prophet

saith, I will go before thee and will lay low the *Is. xlv. 2.*
mountains. And I will break the doors of brass
and burst the bars of iron; and I will give unto
thee the treasures of darkness hidden and unseen,
that they may know that I am the Lord God; and,
He shall dwell in the lofty cave of the strong rock.
Then what saith he of the Son? His water is sure. *Is. xxxiii. 16.*
Ye shall behold the king in his glory, and your
soul shall practise the fear of the Lord. And again
in another prophet he saith, He that doeth these *Ps. i. 3—6.*
things shall be as a tree that groweth beside a
water-course, which giveth his fruit in his season;
and his leaf shall not fall off and whatever he doeth
shall prosper. Not so are the ungodly, not so;
they are like the dust which the wind carrieth away
from the face of the earth, wherefore the ungodly
shall not rise up in judgment, nor sinners in the
congregation of the just: for the Lord knoweth the
way of the just, but the way of the ungodly shall
perish. Ye perceive how he hath put together the
water and the cross. For what he meaneth is this,
Blessed are they who having hoped on the cross
have gone down into the water. For he
speaketh of a reward to be given at the due
season; then, saith he, I will render what is
due unto you. But now in that he saith, Their
leaves shall not fall off, he meaneth this, That
every word that goeth out from your mouth in faith
and love shall be for a refuge and a hope unto
many. And again another prophet saith, And the *Zeph. iii. 19.*
land of Jacob was praised beyond the whole earth.

By so saying he meaneth this, He shall glorify the vessel that containeth his Spirit. And what sayeth he afterwards? There was a river flowing on the right, and there grew up on its banks fair trees, and he who eateth of them shall live for ever. By this he meaneth that we go down into the water full of sin and pollution, and go up bearing fruit in the heart, having in the spirit fear and hope toward Jesus. And whoever shall eat of them shall live for ever. He meaneth this, Whoever, he saith, shall hear these words spoken and believe them shall live for ever.

XII.

In like manner again he signifieth concerning the cross in another prophet, who saith, And when shall these things be fulfilled? The Lord saith, When the tree hath been bent and shall rise up again, and when blood shall flow from the tree. You have again a prophecy concerning the cross and about him who is about to be crucified. And he saith again in Moses, when Israel was being made war upon by aliens, even that he might remind them while they were being made war upon that for their sins they were being delivered over unto death, the Spirit saith unto the heart of Moses that he should make the form of a cross, and of him who was about to suffer, signifying thereby that if they hope not upon him they will be made war upon for ever. Moses, therefore, placeth one weapon upon another in the midst of the fight, and standing higher than all, stretched out his hands, and so again Israel conquered; then, when he let them down, they were again slaughtered. Wherefore? that they might know that they are not to be saved except they hope upon him. And again in another prophet he saith, All day long have I stretched out my hands unto a people who are disobedient, and who speak against my righteous way. Again Moses maketh another type of Jesus, that it behoveth that he should suffer and cause others to live, whom they thought that they had destroyed in figure when Israel was falling: For the Lord made every kind of snake to bite them, and they died, since the transgression happened to Eve by means of the serpent, to the end that he might convince them that through their transgression they should be given over to the pangs of death. For in the end Moses himself, after that he had given commandment, There shall not be among you a molten image or a graven image for a god, maketh one himself that he might show a type of Jesus. Moses, therefore, maketh a brazen serpent, and setteth it aloft, and calleth the people by a proclamation. When, therefore, they had come together they besought Moses that he should offer supplication for them concerning their healing. Moses therefore saith unto them, When any of you is bitten let him come unto the serpent, that is placed upon the tree, and let him believe and hope that, though it is dead, it is able to make him live, and immediately he shall be saved; and so did they. You have, therefore, again the glory of Jesus, that in him and to him are all things. What again saith Moses unto Jesus the son of Nun, having given this name to him, being a prophet? Only that all the people might hear that the Father revealeth all things concerning his son. Moses therefore saith unto the son of Nun, having given him this name when he sent him to spy out the land, Take the book into thy hand and write therein what the Lord saith, even that the Son of God, in the last days, will cut off the whole house of Amalek from the roots. Behold, therefore, again Jesus, not the son of man but the Son of God, made manifest by a type in the flesh. Since, therefore, they should one day say that Christ is the son of David, David himself prophesieth, fearing and understanding the deceitfulness of sinners, The Lord said unto my Lord, Sit on my right hand until I make thy enemies thy footstool. And again Esaias speaketh in this wise, The Lord said unto Christ, my Lord, whose right hand I have held, that the Gentiles should hearken before him, and I will break the strength of kings. Behold how David calleth him Lord, and how he calleth him the Son of God.

Ex. xvii. 14.

Matt. xxii. 43.

Ps. cx. 1.

Isaiah xlv. 1.

XIII.

Let us inquire, therefore, whether this people or the first people inheriteth, and whether the covenant is unto us or unto them. Hear, now, what the scripture saith concerning the people.

But Isaac prayed for Rebecca his wife because she Gen. xxv. 21.
was barren, and she conceived. Then went forth
Rebecca to inquire of the Lord, and the Lord said
unto her, Two nations are in thy womb, and two Gen. xxv. 23.
peoples are in thy bowels, and the one people
shall surpass the other, and the elder shall serve
the younger. Ye ought to understand who was
Isaac and who was Rebecca, and concerning whom
he declared that the one people was greater than
the other. And in another prophecy Jacob speaketh
yet more clearly to Joseph his son, saying, Behold Gen. xlviii. 9,
the Lord hath not deprived me of thy face ; bring 11.
unto me thy sons, that I may bless them. And
he brought unto him Ephraim and Manasseh,
wishing that he should bless Manasseh, because
he was the elder. Joseph, therefore, brought him
to the right hand of his father Jacob. But Jacob
saw in spirit a figure of the people that should be
hereafter. And what saith the scriptures? And
Jacob crossed his hands, and placed his right hand
on the head of Ephraim, the second and youngest,
and blessed him. And Joseph said unto Jacob,
Change thy right hand unto the head of Manasseh,
because he is my first born son. And Jacob said
unto Joseph, I know, my child, I know ; but the
elder shall serve the younger ; but this one also
shall be blessed. Behold in what way he appointed that this people should be the first and heir
of the covenant. If, therefore, it were moreover
mentioned through Abraham also, we have the perfecting of our knowledge. What, therefore, saith he

unto Abraham, when he alone believed, and it was
<small>Rom. iv. 3.
Gen. xv. 6.
xvii. 5.</small> counted unto him for righteousness? Behold I have made thee, Abraham, a father of the nations who believe on the Lord in uncircumcision.

XIV.

Yea; but let us inquire whether he hath given the covenant that he sware unto our fathers that he would give unto the people. Verily he hath given it; but they were not worthy to receive it on <small>Ex. xxiv. 18.</small> account of their sins. For the prophet saith, And Moses was fasting in Mount Sinai forty days and forty nights, that he might receive the covenant which the Lord had made with his people. And <small>Ex. xxxi. 18.</small> he received from the Lord the two tables that were written in the spirit with the finger of the hand of the Lord. And Moses, when he had received them, was bringing them down to the people for to give them. And the Lord said unto Moses, <small>Ex. xxxii. 7.</small> Moses, Moses, get thee down quickly, for thy people, whom thou broughtest out of the land of Egypt, have done unlawfully. And Moses perceived that they had again made molten images, <small>Deut. ix. 12.</small> and he cast the tables from his hands, and the tables of the covenant of the Lord were broken. Moses indeed received them, but the people were not worthy. Hearken ye, therefore, how we have received them. Moses received them being a servant, but the Lord himself gave unto us to be a people of inheritance, having suffered for our sake. And he was made manifest, that both they might be made perfect in their sins, and that we, through him that inherited, might receive the covenant of the Lord Jesus. For; for this purpose was he prepared, that by appearing himself and redeeming from darkness our hearts, which were already consumed by death, and given over to the iniquity of deceit, he might place in us the covenant of his people. For it is written how the Father giveth commandment unto him, that having redeemed us from darkness, he should prepare for himself a holy people. Therefore the prophet saith, I, the Lord thy God, have called thee in righteousness, and I will hold thy hand and make thee strong; and I have given thee for a covenant to the nation, for a light unto the Gentiles, to open the eyes of the blind, and to bring out of chains them that are bound, and from the house of prison them that sit in darkness. Learn, therefore, from whence we were redeemed. And again, the prophet saith, Behold, I have placed thee for a light unto the Gentiles, that thou shouldst be for a salvation unto the end of the earth; thus saith the Lord God who hath redeemed thee. And again the prophet saith, The Spirit of the Lord is upon me, because he hath anointed me; he hath sent me to preach the gospel unto the poor, to heal those that are broken in heart, to preach deliverance to the captives, and the recovery of sight to the blind, to tell of the acceptable year of the Lord, and the day of recompense, to comfort all that mourn.

XV.

And, moreover, concerning the sabbath it is written in the ten commandments, in which he spake on Mount Sinai unto Moses face to face: <small>Exo. xx. 8. Deut. v. 12.</small> Sanctify ye the sabbath of the Lord with pure hands and a pure heart. And in another place <small>Jer. xvii. 24.</small> he saith, If my sons shall keep my sabbath, then will I place my mercy upon them. He speaketh, too, of the sabbath in the beginning of the creation: <small>Gen. ii. 2.</small> And God made in six days the works of his hands, and finished them on the seventh day, and rested in it and sanctified it. Consider, my children, what signify the words, He finished them in six days. They mean this: that in six thousand years the Lord will make an end of all things, for a day is with him as a thousand years. And he himself beareth witness unto me, saying: <small>Ps. xc. 4.</small> Behold this day a day shall be as a thousand years. Therefore, my children, in six days, that is in six thousand years, shall all things be brought to an end. And the words, He rested on the seventh day, signify this: After that his Son hath come, and hath caused to cease the time of the wicked one, and hath judged the ungodly, and changed the sun and the moon and the stars, then shall he rest well on the seventh day. And further he <small>Is. i. 13.</small> saith, Thou shalt sanctify it with pure hands and a pure heart. Who, then, can sanctify the day which the Lord hath sanctified, unless he be pure of heart? If, therefore, we think that any one can sanctify the day that the Lord hath sanctified, unless he be pure of heart in all things, we are deceived. Behold, therefore, who it is that resteth properly and sanctifieth it; even when we ourselves, having first been sanctified, having been justified, and having received the promise, when iniquity exists no longer, but all things have become new, we shall be able to sanctify it. And, further, he saith unto them, Your new moons and your sabbaths I cannot endure. See, now, what he meaneth. Your sabbaths, as they now are, are not acceptable unto me, but that which I have made is, even that in which, after that I have brought all things to an end, I shall make a beginning of the eighth day, which thing is the beginning of another world. Wherefore we keep the eighth day as a day of gladness, on which also Jesus rose from the dead, and after he had appeared ascended unto heaven.

XVI.

And I will, moreover, tell you concerning the temple, how these wretched men, being deceived, placed their hopes in the building as if it were the habitation of God, and not on God who had made them. For almost after the manner of the Gentiles did they consecrate him in the temple. But what saith the Lord, making it of none effect? Hearken ye: Who hath measured out the heaven with his Is. xl. 12.

palm, or the earth with the flat of his hand, is it not I? saith the Lord. Heaven is my throne, and earth the footstool of my feet. What house will ye build for me, or what shall be the place of my rest? Hence ye may know that their hope is vain. And yet further he sayeth again, Behold they that have destroyed this temple shall rebuild it. And so doth it happen, for through their wars it was destroyed by the enemy, and now both they themselves and their enemies shall rebuild it. And again it was made manifest how the temple and the people of Israel should be given up to their enemies. For the scripture saith, And it shall come to pass in the last days that the Lord shall deliver up the sheep of his pasture, and their fold and their cover shall he give up to destruction; and it happened according to that which the Lord had spoken. Let us inquire, therefore, whether there be any temple of God. There is; even where he himself hath declared that he would make and perfect it. For it is written, And it shall be when the week is completed that the temple of the Lord shall be built gloriously in the name of the Lord. I find, therefore, that there is a temple, but how shall it be built in the name of the Lord? Before that we believed in God the habitation of our heart was corrupt and feeble, as being of a truth a temple built by hands. For it was full of idolatry, and was a habitation of devils, because we did such things as were contrary to God; but it shall be built in the name of the Lord. What mean these words? Attend ye: that the temple of the Lord may be built gloriously. But in what manner? Learn ye: having received the remission of our sins, and having hoped upon the name of the Lord, we have become new, having been again created entirely. Wherefore, God of a truth dwelleth in us as in an habitation. How? The word of his faith, the calling of his promise, the wisdom of his ordinances, the commandments of his doctrine, he himself prophesying in us, he himself dwelling in us. To us, who were enslaved by death, he openeth the gate of the temple, which is his mouth, and, giving us repentance, leadeth us into the temple incorruptible. For he who desireth to be saved looketh not unto man, but unto him that dwelleth and speaketh in man, wondering that he had never heard him speaking such words out of his mouth, or even desired to hear. This is the spiritual temple built by the Lord.

XVII.

So far as it is possible for me to show you these things with simplicity, my mind and soul hopeth that I have not omitted any of the things that pertain unto salvation; for if I write unto you concerning the things that are at hand, or the things that will be hereafter, ye would not be able to understand them, because they are couched in parables. These things, therefore, are thus.

XVIII.

Let us pass on now to another kind of knowledge and instruction; for there are two paths of instruction and authority—the one that of light, and the other that of darkness. But there is a great difference between the two paths. For over the one are appointed as illuminators the angels of God, over the other the angels of Satan; on the one side is he who is Lord from everlasting to everlasting, on the other is the ruler of the world that now lieth in wickedness.

XIX.

Now, the path of life is this: If any one wishes to travel to the appointed place, let him hasten by means of his works. Now, the knowledge of walking herein that is given unto us is of this kind: Thou shalt love him that made thee, thou shalt fear him that formed thee, thou shalt glorify him that redeemed thee from death. Thou shalt be simple in heart, and rich in spirit; thou shalt not cleave unto them that go in the path of death. Thou shalt hate whatever is not pleasing unto God; thou shalt hate all hypocrisy; thou shalt not abandon the commandments of the Lord; thou shalt be humble in all things; thou shalt not take glory unto thyself; thou shalt not take evil counsel against thy neighbour, thou shalt not take audacity into thy soul. Thou shalt not commit fornication, thou shalt not commit adultery. Thou shalt not pollute thyself with mankind: let not the word of God go forth from thee in corruption. Thou shalt not accept the person of any man when thou reprovest him for transgression. Thou shalt be gentle, thou shalt be quiet; thou shalt tremble at the words that thou hast heard; thou shalt not bear malice against thy brother; thou shalt not doubt whether a thing shall be or not; thou shalt not take the name of the Lord in vain. Thou shalt love thy neighbour beyond thine own soul; thou shalt not kill a child by abortion, neither shalt thou destroy it after it is born. Thou shalt not remove thy hand from thy son or thy daughter, but shalt teach them from their youth the fear of the Lord. Thou shalt not covet thy neighbour's goods, thou shalt not be an extortioner; neither shall thy soul cleave unto the ground, but thou shalt have thy conversation with the lowly and the just. Receive as blessings the troubles that come unto thee, knowing that without God nothing happens. Thou shalt not be double-minded nor double-tongued; for to be double-tongued is the snare of death. Thou shalt submit thyself to thy masters as to the image of God, with shame and fear. Thou shalt not give commands with bitterness to thy servant and thy handmaid, who hope in the same God as thou dost, lest, perchance, thou cease to fear God, who is over both. For he came not to call men with respect of persons, but to call those whom the spirit had prepared. Thou shalt communicate in all things with thy neighbour, and shalt not say that things are thine own. For if ye be partners in that which is incorruptible, how much more in the things that are corruptible? Thou shalt not be hasty of speech, for the mouth is a snare of death. As far as thou art able thou shalt be pure concerning thy soul. Be not a stretcher forth of thy hand in receiving, and a drawer back of it in giving. Thou shalt love, as the apple of thine eye, every one that speaketh unto thee the word of the Lord. Thou shalt remember the day of judgment by night and by day; and thou shalt seek out every day the persons of the saints. Thou shall not doubt to give, nor shalt thou murmur in giving. Give to every one that asketh thee, and thou shalt know who is the good recompenser of the reward. Thou shalt take care of that which thou hast received, neither adding thereto, or taking therefrom. Thou shalt hate the evil man unto the end, and shalt judge justly. Thou shalt not make a schism, but shalt make peace by bringing adversaries together. Thou shalt make confession of thy sins. Thou shalt not go unto prayer with an evil conscience. This is the way of life.

XX.

But the path of darkness is crooked and full of cursing, for it is the path of eternal death and punishment, in which way are the things that destroy the soul. Idolatry, boldness, the pride of power, hypocrisy, double-heartedness, adultery, murder, rape, haughtiness, transgression, deceit, malice, self-will, witchcraft, sorcery, covetousness, want of the fear of God. Here are they who are persecutors of the good, haters of truth, lovers of lies; they who know not the reward of righteousness, who cleave not to what is good nor unto just judgment; who attend not to the widow and the orphan; who are awake not unto the fear of God, but unto evil; from whom meekness and patience are afar off; who love the things that are vain, who follow after recompense, who pity not the poor, who labour not for him who is in trouble; who are prompt to evil-speaking, who know not him that made them; murderers of children, corruptors of the image of God; who turn away from the poor man and oppress the afflicted; advocates of the rich, unjust judges of the poor, sinners in all things.

XXI.

It is therefore right that he who has learned the ordinances of the Lord, even as many as have been written beforehand, should walk in them. For he who doeth these things shall be glorified in the Kingdom of God, but he who hath chosen the contrary things shall perish together with his works. On this account is the resurrection; on this account is the retribution. I ask those who are of high estate among you, if ye will receive any friendly advice from me, to keep among you those to whom you may do good and desert them not.

Abandon not that which is good; for the day is at hand in which everything shall perish together with the evil one; for the Lord is nigh at hand and his reward is with him. And yet once more do I ask you, be ye good law-givers. Abide faithful counsellors of one another; take out of the midst of you all hypocrisy, and may God, who ruleth the whole world, give you wisdom, understanding, science, knowledge of his ordinances, and patience. And be ye taught of God, inquiring what the Lord seeketh of you, and so work that ye may be found saved in the day of judgment. But if there is any memory of that which is good, remember me while ye practise these things, that both your desire and your watching may turn unto some good. I beseech you this, asking it as a favour. So long as this good vessel is with you, fail not in any of these things, but seek them out without ceasing, and fulfil all the commandments, for these things are worthy. Therefore I have been the more anxious to write unto you, so far as I was able, to the end that I might make you glad. Farewell, children of love and peace; the God of glory and of all grace be with your spirit. Amen.

The Epistles of S. Ignatius.

The Epistle of S. Ignatius to the Ephesians.

IGNATIUS, who is also called Theophorus, to the Church which is at Ephesus in Asia, deservedly thought happy, blessed in the greatness and fulness of God the Father, predestinated before the world for a glory abiding, not to be overturned, united and elect in the true passion of Christ, by the will of the Father and of Jesus Christ our God, much joy in Jesus Christ and in blameless grace.

I.

I have heard in God of your much beloved name, according to the faith and love in Jesus Christ, that being imitators of God, and having refreshed yourselves in the blood of God, ye have perfected completely the work akin to your nature. For when ye heard that I had come bound from Syria on behalf of our common name and hope, hoping that by your prayers I should obtain to fight with wild beasts at Rome, that I might be able, through martyrdom, to attain to being a disciple of him who offered himself for us as an offering and sacrifice unto God. Since, therefore, I have received your abundance in Onesimus, in the name of God, a man of inexpressible love, and your bishop according to the flesh; whom I beseech by Jesus Christ that ye love, and that ye all be like unto him. Blessed is he who hath granted unto you, who are worthy, to obtain such a bishop.

II.

But concerning my fellow servant Burrhus, who is, according to God, your minister, blessed in all things, I pray that he may abide unto your honour and to that of the bishop. And Crocus, who is worthy of God and of you, whom I have received as an example of your love, hath refreshed me in all things; even so may the Father of our Lord Jesus Christ refresh him, together with Onesimus, and Burrhus, and Euplus, and Phronto, through whom I have seen you all in love. May I be benefited by you continually, if at least I am worthy. It is therefore fitting in every way that ye should glorify Jesus Christ who hath glorified you, to the end that ye should be perfected in one subjection, in the same mind, and in the same spirit, and should all be of one voice concerning the same thing; that being subject to the bishop and the presbyters ye may be perfected in all things.

III.

I give not command unto you as though I were some one. For though I be bound for the name of Christ, I am not yet made perfect in him. For I am now beginning to be a disciple, and speak unto you as being joint teachers of me together with Christ. For it behoved me to be prepared by you—by faith, by admonition, by patience, by long-suffering. But since love suffereth me not to be silent concerning you, on this account have I chosen beforehand to exhort you, that ye should run in harmony with the spirit of God. For of a truth, Jesus Christ, our indiscernible life, is the word of the Father, even as the bishops who are appointed throughout the bounds of the world are by the word of Jesus Christ.

IV.

Whence it becometh you to agree with the opinion of the bishop, as ye also do. For your renowned presbytery, worthy of God, is as harmonious with the bishop as the strings are with the lyre. Wherefore, by your concord and harmonious love is Jesus Christ celebrated ; yea, each of you becometh a band. So that ye, being harmonious in concord, and having received the melody of God in union, sing with one voice unto the Father through Jesus Christ that he also may hear you, and may know from your good deeds that ye are the members of his Son. It is therefore useful that ye should be in blameless unity, that ye may be all partakers of God.

V.

For if I, in a short time, have had such intimacy with your bishop, an intimacy not human but spiritual, how much more do I deem you happy who are thus united to him as the Church is to Jesus Christ, and as Jesus Christ is to the Father, that all things may be harmonious in unity. Let no man be deceived; unless a man be within the altar, he lacketh the bread of God. For if the prayers of one or two have so much power, how much more that of the bishop and the whole Church! He therefore who agreeth not in unity is proud and hath condemned himself. For it is written, God resisteth the proud. Let us therefore be careful not to resist the bishop, that we may be subject unto God.

VI.

And the more one sees a bishop to be silent, so much the more let us reverence him. For every one whom the master of the house sendeth for the management of the house, it is right that we should receive, even as we did him that sent him. It is evident, therefore, that it is right to regard the bishop even as the Lord himself. Onesimus, therefore, himself praiseth above measure your good order in God, that ye live according to truth, that no heresy dwelleth in you. But neither do ye pay attention to any one more than to Jesus Christ speaking in truth.

VII.

For some have been accustomed to bear the name (of Christian) about with evil craft, doing certain other things unworthy of God, whom ye must avoid as ye would wild beasts, for they are mad dogs, biting secretly, whom ye must guard against, since their bite is hard to cure. There is one physician, fleshly and spiritual, born and unborn, God made in the flesh, the true life in immortality, born of Mary and of God, first liable to suffering, and then impassive.

VIII.

Let not therefore any man deceive you, neither indeed are ye deceived, being altogether of God. For when there is no strife woven among you that is able to trouble you, then do ye live according to God. I am the offscouring of you, the purification of the Church of you Ephesians, that is famous through all ages. They who are carnal cannot do the things that are spiritual, nor can the spiritual do the things that are carnal; so neither can faith do the deeds of unbelief, or unbelief of faith. For even the things that ye do according to the flesh they are spiritual, for ye do all things in Jesus Christ.

IX.

But I knew of certain men who had passed from thence unto you, bringing an evil doctrine, whom ye did not suffer to sow among you, but closed your ears so that ye might not receive the things sowed by them. Since ye are stones of the temple of the Father prepared for the building of God; being carried up to the height by the machine of Jesus Christ, even his cross, using as a rope the Holy Spirit, but faith is your pulley and love the way that conducteth you unto God. Ye are therefore all fellow travellers, bearers of God, and bearers of the temple, bearers of Christ, bearers of holy things, adorned in all things with the commandments of Jesus Christ. Wherefore, I rejoice that I was thought worthy to associate with you by the things that I write, and to unite in your joy, because ye love nothing that is according to another life, but God alone.

X.

But pray ye without ceasing for other men also, for there is in them a hope of repentance if they attain to God. Exhort them therefore, that they may be taught at any rate by your deeds. To their wrath do ye show yourselves meek, to their high language be ye humble, to their blasphemies oppose prayers, to their wanderings show yourselves firm in the faith, to their wildness show yourselves mild; not being eager to imitate them. Let us be found their brethren in kindness; but let us be eager to be imitators of the Lord; (for who suffered more injustice, who was more defrauded, who was more set at nought than he?) to the end that no herbage of the devil may be found in you; but that ye should abide in all purity and temperance in Jesus Christ, in flesh and in spirit.

XI.

These are the last times. For the remainder let us be sober; let us fear lest the long-suffering of God become unto us a means of condemnation. Let us either fear the wrath to come, or love the grace that is present—one of these two; only strive to be found in Jesus Christ, so that ye may attain unto the true life. Let nothing be seemly for you apart from him. in whom I bear about the spiritual pearls, my bonds, in which may it be my lot to rise in answer to your prayer. Of this prayer may I ever be a partaker, that I may be found in the lot of the Ephesian Christians, who have always agreed with the Apostles in the power of Jesus Christ.

XII.

I know who I am, and to whom I write. I am condemned, ye have found mercy. I am in danger, ye are firmly established. Ye supply the passage for those who are slain for the sake of God. Ye are the fellow disciples of Paul the sanctified, the martyred, the justly thought happy: in whose footprints may I be found when I attain unto God; even Paul who, in the whole of his epistle, makes mention of you in Jesus Christ.

XIII.

Be diligent therefore to come together more frequently to offer thanksgiving unto God and to glorify him. For when ye frequently come together the power of Satan is destroyed, and his destructive influence is broken up by reason of the unity of your faith. Nothing is better than peace, by which all war, both of things in heaven and things on earth, is brought to an end.

XIV.

But none of these things escape your knowledge if ye have faith and love perfectly in Jesus Christ, which are the beginning and end of life; faith is the beginning and love is the end; and the two, being in unity, are of God. But all the other things are consequent upon goodness. No one who maketh profession of faith sinneth: nor does he who hath acquired love, hate. The tree is known from its fruits, so they who profess to be Christians shall be made manifest by the things that they do. For the work is not now of promise, but in the power of faith, if a man be found faithful unto the end.

XV.

It is better to be silent and to be somewhat, than to speak and to be nought. It is a good thing to teach, if he who preacheth, practiseth. There is one teacher who spake and it was done, and the things that he did silently are worthy of the Father. He who possesseth the word of Jesus is of a truth able to hear even his silence, that he may be perfect; that he may act by means of the things that he speaks, and may be known by the things on which he is silent.

XVI.

Be not deceived, my brethren; the corruptors of families shall not inherit the kingdom of God. If, therefore, they who did these things according to the flesh are dead, how much the more if any one corrupt, by evil teaching, the faith of God for which Christ was crucified! Such an one, being filthy, shall depart unto the unquenchable fire, in like manner with him who hearkeneth unto him.

XVII.

On this account was our Lord anointed upon his head, that he might inspire the Church with incorruption. Be ye not anointed with the evil odour of the teaching of the ruler of the world, lest he lead you captive from the life set before you.

Why are not we all wise, after that we have received the knowledge of God, which is Jesus Christ? Why do we foolishly perish, through ignorance of the gift which the Lord hath truly sent?

XVIII.

My spirit is as it were a sacrifice for the cross, which is unto them that believe not a stumbling-block, but unto us salvation and life everlasting. Where is the wise, where is the disputant, where is the boasting of those who are called prudent? For our God Jesus Christ was conceived by Mary, according to the appointment of God, of the seed of David, and of the Holy Spirit; who was born and baptised that by his sufferings he might purify the water.

XIX.

And the virginity of Mary was hidden from the ruler of this world, and her parturition; and in like manner also the death of the Lord, and the three mysteries of the shout, which were done in the silence of God. How, then, were they made manifest unto the ages? A star in heaven shone out beyond all the stars, and its light was ineffable, and its newness caused astonishment. But all the other stars, together with the sun and moon, became a chorus unto this star, and it was exceeding in its light above them all; and there was a disturbance among them, as to whence came this novelty that was unlike to them. Then all enchantment began to be broken up, every bond of wickedness vanished, ignorance was removed, the ancient kingdom was destroyed, God being manifested in human shape for the newness of eternal life ; and that which was perfected with God received its beginning. Thence all things were moved together, because the extinction of death was devised.

XX.

But if Jesus Christ shall deem me worthy by your prayer, and it be his will, in the second book which I am about to write unto you I will show you still further concerning the dispensation of which I have begun to write with regard to the new man Jesus Christ, in his faith and in his love, in his suffering and in his resurrection.

XXI.

I am ready to give my life for you and for him whom ye have sent for the honour of God to Smyrna, whence also I write unto you, returning thanks unto the Lord, loving Polycarp even as I do you. Remember me even as Jesus Christ remembereth you. Pray for the Church which is in Syria, from whence I am led bound unto Rome, being the last of those that believe there, even as I have been thought worthy to be found to manifest the honour of God. Be strong in God the Father and in Jesus Christ, in one common hope.

The Epistle to the Magnesians.

IGNATIUS, who is also Theophorus, to her that is blessed in the grace of God the Father, in Jesus Christ our Saviour, in whom I salute the Church that is in Magnesia by Mæander, and pray in God the Father and in Jesus Christ that they may rejoice greatly.

I.

Having heard of the abundant good order of your love which is according to God, I have with gladness chosen to address you in the faith of Jesus Christ; for having been deemed worthy of the most God-like name in the bonds I bear about, I celebrate the Churches, in which I pray that there may be the union of the body and spirit of Jesus Christ, our everlasting life, and of faith and love, to which there is nothing preferable, but above all of Jesus and the Father, in whom abiding and escaping all the insults of this world, we shall attain unto God.

II.

Since, therefore, I have been deemed worthy to behold you through Damas, your bishop, who is worthy of God, and your worthy presbyters Bassus and Apollonius, and my fellow servant the Deacon Sotion, of whom may I have joy, because he is subject to the bishop as to the grace of God, and to the presbyters as to the law of Jesus Christ.

III.

And you it beseemeth not to despise the youth of your bishop, but to award all reverence unto him, respecting the power of God the Father which is in him, not having regard to his youth, but as wise men in God yielding unto him : yet not unto him but unto the Father of Jesus Christ, who is bishop of all. It is therefore right that we should obey to the honour of him that hath loved us ; since not only doth a man deceive the visible bishop, but he also sets at naught the invisible one ; but such an one has to give an account not unto the flesh, but unto God, who knoweth the secret things.

IV.

It is therefore fitting not only to be called Christians, but also to be so, and not to be as some who call their bishop a bishop, but do all things apart from him ; but such appear to me not to be of good conscience, since they do not steadfastly assemble themselves together according to the commandment.

V.

Since, therefore, things have an end, the choice of two things, death and life, is placed before us, and each is about to depart to his own place. For as there are two kinds of coins, the one of God, the other of the world, and each hath its own impression, the unbelieving the impress of the world, the believers in love the impress of God the Father through Jesus Christ, through whom unless we attain voluntarily to die unto his passion, there is no life in us.

VI.

Since, then, I have in the persons of those above mentioned beheld as it were your whole multitude in faith and love, I exhort you to be careful to do all things in the unity of God, since the bishop sits in the place of God, and the presbyters in the place of the synod of the Apostles, and the deacons, who are most dear to me, have been entrusted with the ministry of Jesus Christ, who was with the father before the world, and was manifested in the end. Do ye all then, having put on the same divine disposition, have respect one for another, and let no one behold his neighbour according to the flesh, but love each other con-

VII.

As, therefore, the Lord did nothing apart from the Father, neither by himself nor by his Apostles, so neither do ye anything without the bishop and the elders; neither try that anything should appear reasonable to yourselves separately; but let there be in unison one prayer, one supplication, one mind, one hope in love, and in blameless joy. There is one Jesus Christ, than which there is nothing better. Do ye, therefore, come together as unto one temple of God, as unto one Jesus Christ, who came forth from our Father, and is in one, and returned unto one.

VIII.

Be not deceived by heretical opinions, nor by ancient fables, which are unprofitable. For if we live now according to the religion of the Jews, we acknowledge that we have not received grace. For the divine prophets lived according to Christ Jesus. On this account were they also persecuted, who by his grace were inspired to the end, that the disobedient might be fully persuaded that there is one God who manifested himself through Jesus Christ, his son, who is his eternal word, who came not forth from Silence, who in all things was well pleasing to him that sent him.

IX.

If, therefore, they who were under the older dispensation came into a new hope, no longer keeping the Sabbath, but living in observance of the Lord's day, on which day also our life rose through him and through his death, which certain deny, through which mystery we have received faith, (and through this abide, that we may be found disciples of Jesus Christ, our only teacher,) how shall we be able to live apart from him, of whom even the prophets were disciples, and waited for him in the spirit as their teacher? And on this account, he whom they rightly expected, when he came, raised them from the dead.

X.

Let us, therefore, not be insensible to his goodness. For if God shall imitate our actions, we are undone. On this account, being his disciples, let us learn to live according to the religion of Christ. For he who is called by any other name than this is not of God. Lay aside, then, this evil leaven, which hath waxed old and become sour, and change it into a new leaven, which is Jesus Christ. Be ye salted in him, to the end that none of you become corrupt, since by your savour shall ye be tried. It is inconsistent to name the name of Christ Jesus, and to live after the manner of the

XI.

Concerning those things, my beloved, I wished you to be warned beforehand (not because I knew that any of you were so disposed, but as being less than you), so that you fall not into the snares of vainglory, but may be fully persuaded of the birth, the passion, and the resurrection which happened in the time of the governorship of Pontius Pilate, which things were done truly and securely by Jesus Christ, from which hope may none of you be turned away.

XII.

May I have joy of you in all things, if at least I am worthy. For even though I be in bonds, yet I am not to be compared to one of you who are free. I know that ye are not puffed up, for ye have Jesus Christ in yourselves; and still more when I praise you, I know that ye are put to shame, as it is written, The just is his own accuser.

XIII.

Be diligent, therefore, to be confirmed in the doctrine of the Lord and of his Apostles, that ye may be prosperous in all things, whatsoever ye do, both in flesh and spirit, in faith and love, in the Father and the Son, and in the Spirit, in the beginning and the end, together with your most worthily-distinguished bishop, and the nobly woven spiritual crown of your presbytery, and of your deacons, who walk according to God. Submit yourselves to your bishops and to each other, as Jesus Christ to his Father according to the flesh, and the Apostles to Christ, and to the Father, and the Spirit; that there may be a union both fleshly and spiritual.

XIV.

Knowing that ye are full of God, I have exhorted you briefly. Remember me in your prayers that I may attain unto God; and the Church in Syria, whence I am not worthy to be called. For I need your united faith and love in God, that the Church in Syria may be deemed worthy to be refreshed by your Church.

XV.

The Ephesians from Smyrna, from which place also I write unto you, salute you, being present for the glory of God, as also are ye who have in all things refreshed me together with Polycarp, the bishop of the Smyrnæans. And the rest of the Churches salute you for the honour of Jesus Christ. Be strong in the unity of God, possessing his inseparable spirit, which is Jesus Christ.

The Epistle to the Trallians.

IGNATIUS, who is also Theophorus, to the Holy Church which is at Trallis, in Asia, beloved by God, the Father of Jesus Christ, elect and worthy of God, at peace by the flesh and blood and the passion of our Lord Jesus Christ, our hope in the resurrection unto him, which I salute in the fulness, after the Apostolic manner, and pray that it may rejoice greatly.

I.

I have known that you have a disposition blameless and unmovable in patience, not merely for outward use, but in your very nature. Even as Polybius, your bishop, hath showed unto me, who came unto me in Smyrna, according to the will of God and of Jesus Christ, and so rejoiced with me in my bonds in Jesus Christ, that I beheld your whole multitude in him. Having received, therefore, through him your benevolence, which is according to God, I seemed to have found you, as I knew you were imitators of God.

II.

For since ye are subject unto the bishop as unto Jesus Christ, ye appear unto me not to live according to man, but according to Jesus Christ who died for us, that ye, by believing on his death, might escape death. It is necessary, therefore, that ye should do nothing without the bishop, as indeed ye do, and also that ye should submit yourselves to the presbyters as to the Apostles of Jesus Christ our hope, in whom we shall be found walking. It is necessary, also, that the deacons, being ministers of the mysteries of Jesus Christ, should in every way please all men. For they are not ministers of meat and drink, but servants of the Church of God; it is therefore their duty to avoid offences as fire.

III.

In like manner, let all men reverence the deacons, even as Jesus Christ who is the Son of the Father; and the the bishop likewise, and the presbyters as the council of God, and as the bond of the Apostles. Without these there is no Church; concerning which things I am persuaded that it is so with you: for I have received a specimen of your love, and have it with myself in the person of your bishop, whose appearance is great instruction, and whose meekness is strength; whom I reckon that even the ungodly respect, loving him because he spareth not himself.

IV.

I know many things in God, but I measure myself that I may not be lost by boasting; for now is it necessary for me to fear even more, and not to attend to those who puff me up, for they who say such things to me scourge me. Of a truth, I am content to suffer, yet I know not whether I be worthy. For this my zeal, though to many it doth not appear in me, it is in greater force. Therefore I need meekness, by which the ruler of this world is destroyed.

V.

Am I not able to write to you concerning heavenly things? but I fear lest I should cause harm to you, because ye are babes; and (forgive me) lest not being able to receive it, ye be choked. And I, too, not being according to my bonds, but being able to know the things celestial, and the stations of the angels, and the conflicts of principalities, both the things visible and invisible, yet even on that account am still a learner; for many things are lacking to us that we may not fall short of God.

VI.

I therefore exhort you, yet not I but the love of Jesus Christ, to use the Christian food alone, and to abstain from all strange herbage, which is heresy;

[a few words follow which afford no meaning], even as they who administer a deadly drug with honey-wine, which he who knoweth not of it taketh gladly with pleasure, and then receiveth death.

VII.

Guard yourselves, therefore, against such as these, and this will happen unto you if ye be not puffed up, and separate not from our God Jesus Christ, and the bishop, and the commandments of the Apostles. He who is within the altar is pure; that is, he who doeth anything apart from the bishop and the presbytery and the deacons, he is not pure in his conscience.

VIII.

It is not because I have known of anything of the kind in you, but I put you on your guard beforehand because ye are my beloved, foreseeing the snares of the devil. Do ye therefore, having again put on patience, refresh yourselves in faith which is the flesh of the Lord, and love, which is the blood of Jesus Christ. Let none of you have aught against his neighbour; give no opportunities to the Gentiles, that the multitude which is in God may not be blasphemed for the folly of a few, For woe unto him through whose foolishness my Name is blasphemed.

IX.

Be ye deaf, therefore, when any one speaketh unto you apart from Jesus Christ, who is of the race of David, who was born of Mary, who was truly born, ate and drank, was truly persecuted under Pontius Pilate, was truly crucified and died, in the sight of the things that are in Heaven and on earth and under the earth, and was truly raised from the dead, his Father having raised him up; according to the similitude of which also his Father shall raise up those who believe in him; apart from whom we have not the true life.

X.

But if, as certain men who are without God, that is unbelievers, assert, his passion was an appearance, being themselves an appearance, why am I bound, and why do I pray to fight with wild beasts? therefore I die in vain. Of a truth, do I not lie against the Lord?

XI.

Avoid therefore the evil branches that produce deadly fruit, of which if any man taste he dieth forthwith. These therefore are not the planting of the Father, for if they were they would appear branches of the cross, and their fruit would have been incorruptible, through which cross in his passion he exhorteth us who are his members. The body therefore cannot be born apart from the members, since God promiseth union, which is himself.

XII.

I salute you from Smyrna, together with the churches of God who are present with me, who have in all things refreshed me in flesh and in spirit; my bonds exhort you which I bear about for the sake of Jesus Christ, asking that I may attain unto God. Abide in your unity, and in prayers one with another, for it becometh each of you separately, and especially the presbyters, to refresh the bishop unto the honour of Jesus Christ and the Apostles, that I may not be for a testimony against you by writing unto you; and pray ye for me also, who need your love, that I may be thought worthy of the lot to which I press forward to attain, that I may not become a castaway.

XIII.

The love of the Smyrnæans and Ephesians saluteth you. Remember in your prayers the Church which is in Syria, of which I am not worthy to be called bishop, being the last of them. Farewell in Jesus Christ, being subject to the bishop as to the commandment of God; and in like manner also to the presbyters. And do ye each of you love one another with undivided heart. Purify ye my spirit, not only now, but when I attain unto God, for I am still in danger; but the Father in Jesus Christ is faithful to fulfil my request and yours, in whom may ye be found blameless.

The Epistle to the Romans.

IGNATIUS, who is also Theophorus, to the Church that hath obtained mercy in the greatness of the majesty of the most high Father and of Jesus Christ his only son, to her that is beloved and enlightened according to the will of him that willed all things that are, according to the love of Jesus Christ our God, which also presideth in the city and neighbourhood of the Romans, worthy of God, worthy of glory, worthy to be thought happy, worthy of praise, worthy of obtaining her wishes, worthily pure, and presiding in love, bearing the name of Christ, bearing the name of the Father, whom also I salute in the name of Jesus Christ the son of the Father, united both in flesh and spirit to all his commandments, filled with the grace of God without distinction, and purified from all alien colour, much blameless joy in Jesus Christ our God.

I.

Since, in answer to prayer unto God, I have attained to see your faces which are worthy of God, even as I have for a long time asked to receive, having been bound in Jesus Christ. I hope to salute you, if at least it be the will of God that I should be thought worthy to endure unto the end. For the beginning is well arranged, if at least I attain unto grace to receive my lot without hindrance. For I fear your love lest it injure me, for it is easy for you to do what you will; but it is difficult for me to attain unto God, if ye insist upon sparing me.

II.

For I do not desire you to please men, but to please God even as ye do please him. For I shall never again have such an opportunity to attain unto God, nor shall ye be inscribed on a better work, if ye keep silence. For if ye shall be silent concerning me, I shall become a partaker of God; but if ye love my flesh, I shall again have my course to run. Ye can do nothing better for me than that I should be offered unto God, since the altar is now ready. In order that, having formed a band in love, ye may sing unto the Father in Christ Jesus, because God hath deemed me worthy to be found bishop of Syria, having sent for me from the east even unto the west. It is a good thing for me to set from the world unto God, that I may rise unto him.

III.

Ye have never envied any one. Ye have taught others; but I desire that those things which ye have commanded in your teaching should be firmly established. Only seek power for me both from within and from without, that I may not only speak, but may also will; that I may not only be called a Christian, but may also be found one. For if I be found a Christian, I can truly be called one, and then I can be faithful, when I appear no longer to the world. Nothing that appears is eternal. For the things that are seen are temporal, but the things that are not seen are eternal. For our God Jesus Christ, being in the Father, is the more seen. The work is not only one of silence, but Christianity is a matter of greatness.

IV.

I write unto the churches, and charge all that I die willingly for God, if at least ye hinder me not. I entreat you, show not unto me an unreasonable love. Suffer me to be the food of the wild beasts, through whom it is allowed me to attain unto God. I am the corn of God. Let me be ground by the teeth of the wild beasts, that I may be found the pure bread of Christ. Rather encourage ye the beasts, that they may become my tomb, and may leave nothing of my body, that

I may not, after my death, become troublesome to any one. Then shall I be truly a disciple of Christ, when the world shall not even behold my body. Beseech Christ concerning me, that I may be found a sacrifice by means of these instruments. I give not commands unto you, as did Peter and Paul. They were apostles; I am condemned. They were free men; I am even until now a slave. But if I suffer I am the freedman of Christ, and shall live free in him. Now I am learning, being in bonds, to desire nothing [worldly or vain].

V.

From Syria even unto Rome I fight with wild beasts by land and sea, night and day being bound to ten leopards, even the band of soldiers, who even when they receive benefits become the worse. But by their wrong doing I am the more instructed; yet not on this account am I justified. May I have joy of the wild beasts that have been prepared for me, and I pray that they may be found ready for me. I will allure them to devour me quickly, and not to avoid touching me through fear, as they did to some men. And even if they be unwilling and refuse, I will compel them. Pardon me in this. I know what is expedient for me; I am now beginning to be a disciple. Let nothing that is visible or invisible envy me the attaining unto Jesus Christ. May fire and the cross, the attacks of wild beasts [dividings and rend-

VI.

The delights of the world and the kingdoms of this life will profit me nothing. Better is it for me to die unto Jesus Christ than to reign over the ends of the earth. For what is a man profited, if he shall gain the whole world but lose his own soul? I seek him who died for us; him I desire, who rose for us; the pains of birth are come upon me. Pardon me, brethren; do not prevent me from living: do not wish me to die, me who desire to belong to God. Give me not over unto the world. Suffer me to receive the pure light. When I have arrived there I shall be a man of God. Permit me to be an imitator of the suffering of my God. If any one have him in himself, let him know what I mean, and let him sympathise with me, knowing the things that encompass me.

VII.

The ruler of this world desireth to rend me and to corrupt my resolution towards my God. Let not any one of you who are present assist him; rather be ye on my side, that is on the side of God. Speak not of Jesus Christ and desire the world. Let not envy dwell in you; do not even obey me if I should exhort you being present, but rather obey the things that I write unto you. I write unto you alive, desiring to die. My love is crucified, and there is not in me any earthly fire, but living water which speaketh in me, and saith from within, Come hither unto the Father. I delight not in the nurture of corruption, nor in the pleasures of this life. I desire the bread of God, the heavenly bread, the bread of life, which is the flesh of Jesus Christ the Son of God, who was born in the latter time of the seed of David and Abraham. I desire his blood for my drink, which is love incorruptible and everflowing life. I no longer desire to live according to men, and that will be if ye are willing; be willing, therefore, that good will may be showed unto you. I ask you in a few words. Believe me, Jesus Christ will manifest these things unto you, in that I speak truly; even the mouth in which there is no falsehood, by which the Father hath spoken truly. Ask concerning me that I may obtain. I have not written unto you according to the flesh, but according to the will of God. If I suffer, ye have had good will towards me. But if I be rejected from suffering, ye have hated me.

IX.

Remember in your prayer the Church in Syria, which instead of me hath God for its pastor. Jesus Christ alone, and your love, shall be its bishop. But I am ashamed to be numbered among them, for I am not worthy, being the last of them, and one born out of due time. But I have obtained mercy, so that I should be some one if I attain unto God. My spirit saluteth you, and the love of the churches who have received me in the name of Jesus Christ, not as a passer-by. For even those who were not connected with me conducted me from city to city, on my way according to the flesh.

X.

I write unto you from Smyrna by means of the Ephesians, who are worthily thought happy. There is also with me Crocus, the much desired name, together with many others. Concerning those who went before me from Syria unto Rome for the glory of God, I believe that you know them; to whom also ye showed that I was near at hand. For they are all worthy of God and of you, whom it is suitable for you to refresh in every way. I have written these things unto you on the 24th day of August. Fare ye well unto the end in the patience of Jesus Christ. Amen.

The Epistle to the Philadelphians.

IGNATIUS, who is also Theophorus, to the Church of God the Father and the Lord Jesus Christ, which is in Philadelphia, in Asia, to her that hath found mercy and is established in the unity of God, and rejoiceth continually in the suffering of our Lord, and in his resurrection, being fully assured in all mercy, whom I salute in the blood of Jesus Christ, who is an eternal and abiding joy, especially if they be in unity with the bishop, and with the presbyters and deacons, who are with him, who have been made manifest according to the will of Jesus Christ, whom, according to his own will, he hath confirmed and fixed by his Holy Spirit.

I.

I have known that your bishop, not of himself nor through men, hath acquired the ministry that belongeth to the common good, nor yet according to vainglory, but by the love of God the Father and the Lord Jesus Christ, at whose modesty I am ashamed; who, though he is silent, hath more power than they who speak vain things; for he is in harmony with the commandments, as the lyre with its strings. Wherefore my soul deemeth happy his disposition towards God, knowing that it is virtuous and perfect, even his constancy and gentleness in all the moderation of the living God.

II.

Being, therefore, children of light and truth, avoid division and evil teachings; but where the shepherd is, there do ye follow as sheep. For many wolves, which seem worthy of belief, lead captive by evil pleasure them who were running the godly race. But in your unity they shall find no opportunity.

III.

Abstain from evil herbage, which Jesus Christ doth not cultivate, because it is not the planting of the Father. Not that I have found division among you, but thorough purity. For as many as are of God and of Jesus Christ, these are with the bishop; and as many as have repented, and have entered into the unity of the church, these, too, shall be of God, that they may live according to Jesus Christ. Be not deceived, my brethren; if any one followeth a schismatic, he doth not inherit the kingdom of God; if any man walketh in an alien opinion, he agreeth not with the passion of Christ.

IV.

Be diligent, therefore, to use one eucharist, for there is one flesh of our Lord Jesus Christ, and one cup for union with his blood; one altar, even as there is one bishop, together with the presbyters and the deacons, who are my fellow-servants, to the end that whatever ye do, ye may do it according unto God.

V.

My brethren, I am exceedingly poured out in my love for you, and, with joy above measure, I confirm you, yet not I, but Jesus Christ; and though I am in bonds for his sake, I fear the more, as being not yet perfected in suffering. But your prayer unto God shall perfect me, to the end that I may attain unto that lot which, in mercy, hath been given unto me, fleeing unto the gospel as unto the flesh of Jesus, and unto the Apostles as the presbyters of the Church; and let us love the prophets because they were heralds of the gospel, and hoped in him and waited for him; in whom having believed, they were saved in the unity of Jesus Christ, being saints holy and worthy of love and admiration, witnessed to by Jesus Christ, and numbered together in the gospel of the common hope.

VI.

But if any man preach unto you Judaism, hearken not unto him; for it is better to hear Christianity from one circumcised, than Judaism from one uncircumcised. But if both speak not concerning Jesus Christ, then are they in my view tombs and graves, on which are written only the names of men. Avoid, therefore, the evil devices and lyings in wait of the ruler of this world, lest being distressed by his influence, ye become weak in love; but be ye all united in love undivided. I thank my God that I am of a good conscience among you, and that no one is able to boast either secretly or openly that I have been a burden unto any, either in great things or small. I pray that all unto whom I speak may not have this thing as a testimony against them. For even though some have thought that I was a deceiver according to the flesh, yet the spirit, being of God, is not deceived; for he knoweth from whence he cometh, and whither he goeth, and he searcheth out hidden things. I cried while I was among you, and spake with a loud voice, saying, Give heed unto the bishop, and to the presbyters, and to the deacons. But certain of them suspected that I spake these things because I knew beforehand the division of certain of them; but he, for whose name I am in bonds, is witness unto me that I knew not these things through the flesh of man. But the spirit preached, saying these things: Do nothing apart from the bishop; keep your flesh as the temple of God; love unity, avoid divisions; be imitators of Jesus Christ, even as he is of his Father.

VIII.

I therefore performed my proper work, as a man perfectly prepared for unity. For where there is division and anger, God dwelleth not. God, therefore, granteth forgiveness unto all who repent, if they repent in accordance with the unity of God, and the council of the bishop. I trust in the grace of Jesus Christ, who shall loose from you every chain; and I exhort you to do nothing of contention, but according to the discipline of Christ. Since I have heard certain men say, "Unless I find it in the Old (Testament) I believe it not in the Gospel." And when I said unto them that "It is written," they replied, "'That it is set forth aforetime." But my archives are Jesus Christ; his cross and his death, his resurrection, and faith which is through him, are inviolable archives, through which I desire to be justified by means of your prayers.

IX.

Good, too, are the priests: but better is the high priest who is entrusted with the Holy of Holies, who alone is entrusted with the secret things of God: he being the gate of the Father, through which enter Abraham and Isaac, and Jacob, and the prophets, and the apostles, and the church; all these come into the unity of God. But the gospel hath something peculiar; namely, the coming of our Lord Jesus Christ, his suffering, and the resurrection. For the beloved prophets were heralds for him; but the gospel is the perfection of incorruption. All things are good alike, if ye believe in love.

X.

Since, according to your prayer and the mercies which ye have in Christ Jesus, it hath been announced unto me that the Church that is at Antioch, in Syria, is at peace, it is becoming unto you, as unto a church of God, to elect a deacon to go there as an ambassador of God; so that, when ye are together, ye may rejoice with them and glorify the name. Blessed in Jesus Christ is he who shall be deemed worthy of this ministry, and ye shall be glorified. Now, if ye are willing to do this on behalf of the name of God, it is not impossible; even as the churches that are nearest, some sent bishops, and others presbyters and deacons.

XI.

But concerning Philo, the deacon from Cilicia, a man having a good report, who now in the word of God serveth me together with Rheus Agathopus, a chosen man who accompanieth me from Syria, having bid farewell to his life, who also bear witness unto you; and I give thanks unto God on your behalf, that ye received them as the Lord received you. But may they who dishonoured them be redeemed by the grace of Jesus Christ. The love of the brethren in Troas saluteth you; whence also I write unto you by means of Burrhus, who was sent to me jointly by the Ephesians and Smyrnæans as a mark of honour. The Lord Jesus Christ on whom they hope shall honour them in flesh and in sprit, in faith, love, and unity. Fare ye well in Jesus Christ, our common hope.

The Epistle to the Smyrnaeans.

IGNATIUS, who is also Theophorus, to the Church of God the Father and of Jesus Christ the beloved, to her who hath by mercy obtained every gift, filled with faith and love, not lacking in any gift, most godlike, and the mother of saints, to her which is at Smyrna in Asia, much joy in the blameless spirit and word of God.

I.

I glorify God even Jesus Christ, who hath thus made you wise, for I perceived that ye were perfected in immovable faith, as though ye were nailed to the cross of our Lord Jesus Christ in flesh and in spirit, and firmly fixed in love in the blood of Christ, being fully persuaded with regard to our Lord, that he was truly of the race of David according to the flesh, the Son of God according to the will and power of God; truly born of a virgin; baptized by John that all righteousness might be fulfilled by him; truly nailed for us unto the cross in the flesh in the time of Pontius Pilate and Herod the tetrarch; from the fruit of which cross are we from his divinely-blessed passion, that he might raise up a sign unto the ages, even unto the saints and them who believe in him, whether they be among the Jews or the Gentiles, in one body of his church.

II.

All these things did he suffer for our sake, to the end that we might be saved. And he truly suffered, even as he truly raised himself up; not as certain unbelievers say, that he suffered in semblance, they themselves only existing in semblance; and even according to their opinions shall it happen unto them, since they are bodiless and of the nature of devils.

III.

For I also, after his resurrection in the flesh, know him and believe that he is. For when he came unto them who were with Peter he said unto them, Take, handle me, and see that I am not a spirit without a body; and straightway they touched him and believed, being convinced by his flesh and his spirit. On this account also they despised death, and were found superior to death. But after his resurrection, as being in the flesh, he ate and drank with them, though spiritually he was united to the Father.

IV.

These things do I exhort you, beloved, knowing that such is your faith. But I put you on your guard against beasts in human shape, whom not only doth it behove you not to receive, but, if it is possible, not even to meet. But only pray for them, if by any means they may repent; and this is difficult, but it is in the power of Jesus Christ, our true life. For if these things were done by our Lord only in appearance, then in appearance only am I bound. And why have I given myself up unto death, to fire, to sword, to wild beast? but nearness to the sword is nearness to God; to be among the wild beasts is to be in the arms of God; only in the name of Jesus Christ, that I may suffer together with him, I endure all things, since he who became perfect man strengtheneth me.

V.

Whom some in ignorance deny, but have rather been denied of him, being advocates of death rather than of the truth. Whom the prophets have not convinced, nor the law of Moses, nor until now the gospel, nor the sufferings which each of us severally have endured, for of a truth they think that our sufferings also are in appearance. For how doth a man benefit me, if he praise me but blasphemeth my Lord, not confessing that he lived in the flesh? But he who sayeth not this, hath denied him completely, being a bearer of the dead. But it hath not seemed good unto me to write their names, which are those of unbelievers; but may it not even happen unto me to remember them until they repent of their errors with regard to the passion, which is our resurrection.

V.

Let no man be deceived. Even the heavenly things, and the glory of the angels, and the principalities, both visible and invisible, if they believe not on the blood of Christ, for them also is there condemnation. Let him who can receive it, receive it. Let not high place puff up any man. For the whole matter is faith and love, to which there is nothing preferable. Consider those who hold heretical opinions with regard to the grace of Jesus Christ which hath come unto us, how opposite they are to the mind of God.

VI.

They have no care for love, nor concerning the widow, nor concerning the orphan, nor concerning the afflicted, nor concerning him who is hungry or thirsty. They refrain from the eucharist and from prayer, because they do not confess that the eucharist is the flesh of our Saviour Jesus Christ, who suffered for our sins, whom the Father of his goodness raised up.

VII.

They, therefore, who speak against this gift of God, die disputing. But it were better for them to love, that they may rise again. It is, therefore, proper to abstain from such, and not to speak concerning them, either in private or in public; but to attend to the prophets, and especially to the gospel, in which the passion hath been revealed unto us, and the resurrection hath been perfected.

VIII.

But avoid divisions, as being the beginning of evils. Do ye all follow the bishop, as Jesus Christ doth the Father; and follow the presbyters as the apostles; and have respect unto the deacons as unto the commandment of God. Let no one, apart from the bishop, do any of the things that appertain unto the church. Let that eucharist alone be considered valid which is celebrated in the presence of the bishop, or of him to whom he shall have entrusted it. Wherever the bishop appear, there let the multitude be; even as wherever Christ Jesus is, there is the Catholic Church. It is not lawful either to baptize, or to hold a love-feast without the consent of the bishop: but whatsoever he shall approve of, that also is well pleasing unto God, to the end that whatever is done may be safe and sound.

IX.

It is reasonable for the future to be vigilant, and while we have yet time to repent unto God. It is well to honour God and the bishop; he who honoureth the bishop is honoured of God; he who doeth anything without the knowledge of the bishop, serveth the devil. Let all things abound unto you in grace, for ye are worthy. Ye have refreshed me in all things, and Jesus Christ hath refreshed you. Ye have loved me both when absent and present. May God requite you, through whom, by enduring all things, ye shall attain unto him.

X.

Ye have done well in that ye have received as servants of God Philo and Rheus Agathopus, who have followed me for the sake of God; who also return thanks unto the Lord in your behalf, because ye have refreshed them in every way. Nothing shall be lost unto you. My spirit is given for yours, and my bonds, which ye have not despised, nor have been ashamed of them; nor shall perfect faith, even Jesus Christ, be ashamed of you.

XI.

Your prayer hath come unto the Church which is at Antioch in Syria, whence I salute all, being

bound with the most godlike bonds, not being
worthy to be from thence, being the last of them.
But according to his will, I was thought worthy,
not from any merit of which I am conscious, but
of the grace of God, which I pray may be given
unto me in perfection, that, by means of your
prayer, I may attain unto God. In order, therefore, that your work may be perfect, both on earth
and in heaven, it is fitting that your church should
elect a divine ambassador to the honour of God,
that when he come unto Syria he may congratulate
them that they are at peace, and have received
their proper greatness, and their own body hath been
restored unto them. It hath, therefore, appeared
unto me to be a worthy thing to send some of
yours with the epistle, that he may glorify together
with you the prosperity which hath happened unto
them in accordance unto God, and because that
by your prayer it hath already attained unto the
harbour. Since ye are perfect, think also such
things as be perfect; for if ye are willing to do
well, God is ready to grant you the opportunity.

XII.

The love of the brethren who are in Troas
saluteth you, whence also I write unto you by
means of Burrhus, whom ye, together with the
Ephesians your brethren, sent along with me, who
hath in all respects refreshed me; and would that
ye all imitated him, who is a pattern of the service

of God. Grace shall requite you in all things;
I salute also your bishop, who is worthy of God,
and your godlike presbyters, the deacons, who are
my fellow servants, and all of you, both individually
and in common, in the name of Jesus Christ, and
in his flesh and blood, in his passion and resurrection, both fleshly and spiritual, in the name in the
unity both of God and of yourselves. Grace be
unto you, mercy, peace, and patience for ever.

XIII.

I salute the families of my brethren, together
with their wives and children, and the virgins who
are called widows. Fare ye well in the power of
the spirit. Philo, who is with me, saluteth you. I
salute the house of Tavias, whom I pray may be
fixed in faith and love, both fleshly and spiritual.
I salute Alce, the name desired by me, and
Daphnus the incomparable, and Eutienus, and all
by name. Farewell in the grace of God.

The Epistle to Polycarp.

IGNATIUS, who is also Theophorus, to Polycarp, the bishop of the Church of the Smyrnæans, but who rather hath God the Father and the Lord Jesus Christ for his bishop, much joy.

I.

Knowing with approval thy mind, which is in God, fixed as it were upon an immovable rock, I glorify God above measure, having been deemed worthy of thy blameless countenance, of which may I have joy in God. I exhort thee, by the grace with which thou hast been endued, to apply unto thy course, and to exhort all men that they may be saved. Vindicate thy position with all diligence, both of flesh and spirit. Have a care for unity, than which there is nothing better. Support all men, even as the Lord supporteth thee. Bear in love with all men, even as thou doest; give thyself unto prayer without ceasing. Ask for more knowledge than thou hast. Watch, since thou hast obtained a spirit that doth not slumber. Speak unto men separately, as God helpeth thee; bear the infirmities of all men, as a perfect athlete. Where the toil is greater, the gain is great.

II.

If thou love the good disciples, there is no thank for thee; rather by meekness keep in subjection the worse. Every wound is not cured by the same salve; allay irritation by soothing application. Be wise as a serpent in all things, and harmless as a dove. On this account art thou both fleshly and spiritual, that thou mightest soothe the things that appear before thy face. Ask that the invisible things may be made manifest unto thee; that thou mayest lack nothing, and mayest abound in every gift. The time demandeth thee, even as the pilots demand winds, and he who is tempest-tossed demandeth the harbour, that thou shouldest attain unto God. Be sober, as an athlete of God. Thy prize is immortality and life everlasting, concerning which thou also art persuaded. In all things my soul is for thine, and my bonds which thou hast loved.

III.

Be not astounded at those who seem worthy of credit, and yet preach false doctrine. Stand firm, as an anvil which is smitten. It is the part of a

great athlete to be struck and yet to conquer; and
especially it becometh thee to endure everything
for the sake of God, that he also may endure us.
Be yet more zealous than thou art; consider the
times; expect him who is above time, the eternal,
the invisible, who became visible for our sakes,
the intangible, the impassive, who suffered for our
sakes, who for our sakes endured in every way.

IV.

Let not the widows be neglected; be thou next
after the Lord a carer for them: let nothing be
done without thy consent, nor do thou do any
thing apart from God; which neither dost thou do,
being constant. Let your assemblings together be
more frequent. Summon all by name. Do not
despise the male or female slaves; but neither let
them be puffed up; but let them serve the more
diligently unto the glory of God, that they may
attain to a better liberty from God. Let them not
desire to be set free at the common expense, that
they may not become the slaves of concupiscence.

V.

Avoid evil arts, but rather make thy discourse
concerning these things. Charge my sisters, that
they love the Lord, and be content with their
husbands, both in flesh and in spirit. In like
manner, exhort my brethren in the name of Jesus

Christ, that they love their wives, even as the Lord loveth the church. If any one is able to remain in purity as regards the flesh, to the honour of the Lord, let him remain so without boasting; but if he boast he is undone, and if he become of higher estimation than the bishop he is corrupted. It is proper for husbands and wives to make their union with the consent of the bishop, that their marriage may be according to God, and not according to lust. Let everything be done to the honour of God.

VI

Give heed unto the bishop, that the Lord also may give heed unto you. My life is for those who submit to the bishop, the priests, and the deacons; may it happen to me to have my portion with them in God. Labour ye in union with each other; struggle together, run together, suffer together, sleep together, rise together, as stewards of God, as assessors, and servants; please him in whose service ye are soldiers, from whom also ye obtain your pay. Let not one of you be found a deserter. Let your baptism be for you as arms, your faith as a helmet, love as a spear, patience as a panoply. Let your savings be your works, in order that ye may receive your due. Be patient, therefore, with each other in meekness, even as God is with you. May I have joy of you for ever.

VII.

Since the church which is at Antioch in Syria is at peace in answer to your prayer, even as hath been showed unto me, I too have become more joyous in the freedom from care, which is of God, if so be I through suffering may attain unto God, that I may be found ~~in~~ your ~~resurrection~~ a disciple of God. It becometh thee, O Polycarp, most worthy of divine happiness, to collect a most god like council, and to elect some one of you who is much beloved and unwearied in toil, who shall be able to be called the messenger of God. Him should ye deem worthy that he should go into Syria and glorify your unwearied love, which is the glory of Christ. A Christian hath not authority over himself, but his time is given unto God. This is the work of God, and your work, when ye shall have perfected it for him. For I trust that ye are ready by grace for the well-doing that appertaineth unto God. Knowing, therefore, your zeal for the truth, I have exhorted you in a short epistle.

VIII.

Since I have not been able to write unto all the churches, owing to my sailing suddenly from Troas to Neapolis, even as the will of God commandeth, thou, as being possessed of the counsel of God, shalt write unto the neighbouring churches, that they should do the same things. Let those who are able send messengers on foot, let others send epistles by the hands of those who are sent by thee, that ye may be glorified eternally, even as thou art worthy. I salute all by name, and the widow of Epitropus, with her household and her children; I salute Attalus my beloved; I salute him who is about to be deemed worthy to proceed unto Syria; grace shall be with him for ever, and with Polycarp who sendeth him. I pray that ye may be strong for ever in our God Jesus Christ, in whom may ye remain in the unity and supervision of God. I salute Alce, the name desired by me. Farewell in the Lord.

The Epistle of Polycarp

The Epistle of Polycarp to the Philippians.

POLYCARP, and the presbyters who are with him, to the Church of God that sojourneth at Philippi; mercy and peace be multiplied unto you from God Almighty and the Lord Jesus Christ our Saviour.

I.

I rejoiced exceedingly together with you in our Lord Jesus Christ, because ye have received the patterns of true love, and have conducted, even as became you, those who were bound with holy chains, which are the diadems of those who have been truly chosen by God and our Lord; and because the firm root of your faith, which was proclaimed from ancient times, remaineth even until now, and beareth fruit unto our Lord Jesus Christ, who for our sakes endured to proceed even unto death, whom God raised up, having loosed the pains of hell. On whom, not having seen, ye

Acts ii. 24.
1 Pet. i. 8.

believe, and believing rejoice with joy unspeakable and full of glory; unto which many desire to enter in, knowing that by grace ye are saved, not of works, but by the will of God through Jesus Christ.

Ephes. ii. 8

II.

Wherefore, having girt up your loins, serve God in fear and truth, having abandoned vain babbling and the seducing of the many, believing upon him who raised our Lord Jesus Christ from the dead, and gave unto him glory and a throne on his right hand; to whom all things have been made subject, both in heaven and in earth, whom everything that breathes serveth, who is coming as the judge of quick and dead, whose blood God shall require from those who disobey him. But he who raised him from the dead shall also raise us up if we do his will and walk in his commandments, and love the things that he loved, abstaining from all unrighteousness, covetousness, love of money, slander, false witness, not rendering evil for evil, or railing for railing, or blow for blow, or curse for curse, remembering the things of which our Lord spake in his teaching. Judge not that ye be not judged; forgive and it shall be forgiven unto you; show mercy that ye may obtain mercy; with whatsoever measure ye meet it shall be measured unto you again; and that blessed are the poor, and they who are persecuted for righteousness' sake, because theirs is the kingdom of God.

Marginal references: Ephes. vi. 14; Ephes. i. 20; Philipp. ii. 10; 1 Pet. iii. 9; Matt. vii. 1; Luke vi. 37; Matt. vii. 2; Matt. v. 3, 10.

III.

These things, brethren, do I write unto you concerning righteousness, not having taken on myself so to do, but because ye have exhorted me. For neither I, nor any other like unto me, is able to follow the wisdom of the blessed and glorious Paul, who, when he was among you in the presence of the men of that time, taught accurately and surely the word of truth; who even when he was absent, wrote epistles unto you, into which if ye look ye shall be able to be built up with the faith given unto you, which is the mother of us all, hope following, and love of God and Christ and our neighbour going before. For if any one keep within these limits, he hath fulfilled the commandment of righteousness, for he who hath love is far from sin.

IV.

But the love of money is the beginning of all evil. 1 Tim. vi. 10. Knowing, therefore, that we brought nothing 1 Tim vi. 7 into the world, and cannot carry anything out, let us arm ourselves with the arms of righteousness, and teach ourselves first to walk in the commandments of the Lord. Next, teach ye your wives in the faith, and love, and purity given unto them, that they love their own husbands in all truth, and have affection for all men equally in all continence; and to teach your children the education of the fear of God. Teach the widows also that they be sober concerning the faith of the Lord, making intercession without ceasing concerning all men, being far from all slander, evil speaking, false witness, controversy, and all evil; knowing that they are the altar of God, and that all things are under his censure, and that nothing hath escaped him, neither of the reasonings nor the imaginations, nor the secrets of the heart.

V.

Knowing, therefore, that God is not mocked, we ought to walk worthily of his commandment and glory. In like manner let the deacons be blameless before his righteousness, as the deacons of God and Christ, and not of men; not slanderers, not double-tongued, not covetous; temperate in all things, compassionate, careful, walking according to the truth of the Lord, who became the servant of all men, whom if we shall please in the present life, we shall obtain also the life to come; even as he hath promised to raise us from the dead, and that if we walk worthily of him, we shall also reign together with him, if at least we believe. In like manner, also, let the younger men be blameless in all things, above all, having care for purity, and refraining themselves from all evil. It is a good thing to be cut off from the desires that are in the world, because every desire warreth against the spirit, and neither whoremongers, nor effeminate, nor they who defile themselves with mankind, shall inherit the kingdom of God, nor they who do things that are amiss. Wherefore it is right to abstain from all these things, submitting ourselves to the elders and the deacons, as unto God and to Christ. Charge the virgins that they walk in a blameless and pure conscience.

VI.

And let the presbyters be tender-hearted, compassionate towards all men, converting them that have erred, visiting all the sick, not neglecting the widow, or the orphan, or the poor; providing what is honest in the sight of God and man; abstaining from all wrath, respect of persons, unjust judgment; being free from all covetousness, not quickly believing anything against any one, not being harsh in judgment, knowing that we are all debtors of sin. If, therefore, we ask the Lord to forgive us, we ought also to forgive. For we are before the eyes of our Lord and God, and we must all stand before the judgment seat of Christ, and each must give an account of himself. Let us, therefore, thus serve him with fear and all reverence, even as he commanded, and his apostles who preached the gospel unto us, and the prophets who proclaimed beforehand the coming of our Lord.

VII.

1 John iv. 3.   For every one that doth not confess that Jesus Christ is come in the flesh is antichrist; and whosoever doth not acknowledge the testimony of the cross is of the devil; and whosoever alters the oracles of the Lord to suit his own desires, and says that there is neither resurrection or judgment, this man is the first-born of Satan. Wherefore, having abandoned the vanity of the many and their false teaching, let us return unto the word which was delivered unto us from the beginning; watching with prayer and persevering in fasting; asking
Matt. vi. 13. with supplication the all-seeing God not to lead us
Mark xiv. 38. into temptation, even as the Lord hath said, The spirit indeed is willing, but the flesh is weak.

VIII.

Let us, therefore, persevere without ceasing in our hope, and in the earnest of our righteousness,
1 Pet. ii. 24. which is Jesus Christ, who bore our sins in his own body on the tree, who did no sin, neither was guile found in his mouth, but endured all things for our
1 John iv. 9. sake, that we might live in him. Let us, therefore, become imitators of his patience, and if we suffer for his name, let us glorify him; for this example hath he through himself appointed for us, and we have believed this.

IX.

I therefore exhort you all to obey the word of righteousness, and to practise all patience, which also ye see with your eyes, not only in the blessed Ignatius, and Zosimus, and Rufus, but also in the others who are from among you, and in Paul himself, and the rest of the Apostles; being persuaded that thus all ran not in vain, but in faith and righteousness, and that they are now in their appointed place with the Lord, with whom also they suffered; for they loved not the world which now is, but him who died for us, and was for our sakes raised up by God.

X.

Stand therefore in these things, and follow the example of the Lord; be ye firm in the faith and unchangeable, lovers of the brotherhood, kindly affectioned one to another, united in truth, showing the meekness of the Lord to one another, despising no man. Where ye are able to do good, delay it not, for almsgiving freeth from death. Be ye all subject one to another, having your conversation unblameable among the Gentiles, that from your good works ye may both receive praise and the Lord may not be blasphemed among you. But woe unto him through whom the name of the Lord is blasphemed; therefore, teach all men sobriety, in which also ye have your conversation. [1 Pet. v. 5.]

XI.

I was exceedingly sorrowful for Valens, who was sometime made presbyter among you, because he is so ignorant of the position which has been assigned to him. And so I advise you that ye abstain from avarice, and be chaste and truthful; abstain ye from all evil. But if a man is not able to govern himself in these things, how can he tell it to another? If a man abstain not from avarice, he will be stained by idolatry, and will be judged as though he were among the Gentiles. For who are ignorant of the judgment of the Lord? Know we not that the saints shall judge the world, as Paul teacheth? But I have neither perceived nor heard anything of the kind among you, among whom the blessed Paul laboured, who are mentioned in the beginning of his epistles. He boasteth, moreover, concerning you in all the churches which then alone knew God, for we had not yet known him. Therefore, I am exceedingly sorrowful, brethren, both for him and his wife; may the Lord give them true repentance. Be ye also, therefore, moderate in this matter, and regard not such as enemies, but recall them as suffering and erring members, that ye may save the body of all of you, for by doing this ye edify yourselves.

XII.

For I trust that you are well exercised in the Holy Scriptures, and nothing escapes you; but to me at present it is not granted. As it has been said in these Scriptures, Be ye angry and sin not, Ps. iv. 4. let not the sun go down upon your wrath. Blessed Ephes. iv. 26. is he who remembereth this, which thing also I believe to be in you. But may the God and Father of our Lord Jesus Christ, and the everlasting Priest himself, the Son of God Jesus Christ, build you up in faith and truth, and in all meekness and without anger, and in patience and long-suffering and endurance, and chastity, and may he give you your lot and part among his saints, and to us with you, and to all who are under heaven, who are (in time to come) about to believe in our Lord Jesus Christ, and his Father who raised him from the dead. Gal. i. 1. Pray for all saints. Pray also for kings and potentates, and princes, and for them who persecute and hate you, and for the enemies of the cross, that your fruit may be made manifest among all, and that ye may be perfect in him. Both ye and Ignatius wrote unto me that if any one come unto Syria, he should bring away letters from you also. Which thing also I will do, if I find a convenient time, either I or he whom I will send as an ambassador for you also. We have sent unto you the epistles of Ignatius, which were sent unto us by him and others, even as many as we have with us, as ye commanded, which have been placed at the end of this epistle, from which ye will be able to derive great advantage. For they contain faith, and patience, and all the edification that belongeth unto our Lord.

XIII.

I have written unto you these things by Crescens, whom I have commended unto you up to the present day and now commend. For his conversation with us has been blameless, and I believe with you also; ye will receive his sister also in esteem when she cometh unto you. Grace be with you all. Amen.

The Martyrdom of S. Ignatius.

The Martyrdom of S. Ignatius.

I.

WHEN Trajan had not long succeeded to the Roman empire, there lived one Ignatius, the disciple of the apostle St. John, a man in all respects resembling the apostles, and he steered the church of Antioch with diligence, having with difficulty guided it past the former storms of the numerous persecutions under Domitian; like a good pilot, using the helm of prayer and fasting, the oar of teaching, the rope of the spirit, he held out against the opposing storm, fearing lest he should lose any of the more timid and simple brethren. He rejoiced, therefore, at the undisturbed condition of the church when the persecution had for a little ceased; but he was vexed at himself as having not yet attained to real love towards Christ, nor to the true position of a disciple. For he thought that the confession which is made by martyrdom would bring him nearer to the Lord. Wherefore, abiding by the church for a few years longer, and enlightening like a divine lamp the understanding of each by the expounding of Scripture, he attained at last to the things that he desired.

II.

For Trajan after these things, in the ninth year of his reign, being elated with his victory against the Scythians and Dacians and many other nations, and thinking that there still remained wanting to make his dominion entire the God-fearing body of the Christians, and having threatened that unless they were willing to enter into the service of the demons together with all the gentiles, they should undergo persecution, began to compel all who were leading a godly life to sacrifice or to die. Then that noble soldier of Christ, being afraid for the church of Antioch, was led by his own will to Trajan, who was at that period passing his time at Antioch, and hastening towards Armenia and the Parthians. But when he stood before the face of Trajan the king, Who art thou, haunted by an evil demon, that hastenest to transgress our commands, and after to persuade others also, that they may be wretchedly destroyed? Ignatius said, No one calleth him haunted by an evil demon who beareth God about with him, for the demons stand apart from the servants of God. But if, because I am troublesome to them, thou callest me evil towards the demons, I agree; for having

Christ as my King in heaven, I destroy their designs. Trajan said, And who is he that beareth God about with him? Ignatius answered, He who hath Christ in his breast. Trajan said, Do we then seem, in your opinion, not to have Gods whom we use as allies against our enemies? Ignatius replied, Thou art wrong in calling the demons of the gentiles God; there is one God, he who made the heavens and the earth, and the sea and all the things that are in them, and one Jesus Christ the only-begotten Son of God, whose kingdom may I enjoy! Trajan said, Art thou speaking of him who was crucified under Pontius Pilate? Ignatius said, I speak of him who crucified my sin together with the discoverer of it, and hath cast under the feet of those that bear him in their heart all demoniac craft and wickedness. Trajan said, Dost thou, therefore, bear in thy heart the crucified? Ignatius said, Yea, for it is written, I will dwell among them and walk among them. Trajan gave sentence: We have given orders that Ignatius, who sayeth that he beareth about the crucified in himself, should be bound by soldiers and carried to mighty Rome, to be the food of wild beasts for the entertainment of the people. When, therefore, the holy martyr heard this sentence, he cried out with joy: I thank thee, O Master, because thou hast deigned to honour me by perfecting my love unto thee, having bound me with iron bonds together with thy apostle Paul. When he had said these things, he joyfully put on his fetters, having first invoked blessings on the church, and having commended it with tears unto the Lord, like a notable ram, the leader of a fair flock, he was snatched away by the brutal violence of the soldiery, to be carried to Rome for a prey to the blood-devouring wild beasts.

III.

Therefore, with great zeal and joy desiring to suffer, having gone down from Antioch unto Seleucia, he from thence embarked on his voyage. And having, after much toil, put in to the city of the Smyrnæans, having, with great joy, disembarked from the ship, he hastened to behold the holy Polycarp, the bishop of the Smyrnæans, who had been his fellow-hearer of the apostles; for they had been of old disciples of the apostle John; and having been brought to him, and having communicated with him in spiritual gifts, and having gloried in his bonds, he exhorted him to second his purpose, especially exhorting the whole church in common; for the cities of Asia greeted the saint by means of the bishops and presbyters and deacons, all hastening unto him, if by any means they might receive a share of his spiritual gifts; and above all did he exhort S. Polycarp to pray that, by means of the wild beasts, becoming quickly invisible to the world, he might appear before the face of Christ.

IV.

And these things he thus said, and thus testified; so far extending his love towards Christ, as one who was about to attain to heaven by means of his good confession and the zeal of those who prayed together with him on behalf of his conflict, and to pay back the hire to the churches who had met him in the person of their rulers, letters of thanks having been sent out to them, distilling spiritual grace, together with prayer and exhortation. Wherefore, seeing them all favourably disposed towards him, fearing lest the love of the brotherhood might hinder his zeal towards the Lord when an excellent door of martyrdom had been opened unto him, he sendeth to the church of the Romans the following epistle.

Here follows the Epistle of S. Ignatius to the Romans. (See page 129.)

V.

Having, therefore, prepared by his letter the brethren in Rome even as he wished, having thus set sail from Smyrna (for the bearer of Christ was hastened on by the soldiers, that he might arrive before the public games in mighty Rome, in order that, having been delivered to the wild beasts in the sight of the people of the Romans, he might attain to the crown of the contest), he put in to Troas. Then, having been brought from thence to Neapolis through Philippi, he passed by Macedonia, and rounded also that part of the continent which is towards Epidamnus; meeting with a ship in the parts by the sea, he sailed the Adriatic sea, and from thence having embarked upon the Tyrrhenian, and having coasted along the islands and cities, when Puteoli came in sight, the saint was eager to disembark, wishing to walk in the steps of the apostle Paul. But when a violent wind falling upon them did not allow it, the ship being driven forward, after that he had blessed the love of the brethren who were in that place, he so sailed along. Thus, in one day and night, having met with favourable winds, we were carried away unwillingly, lamenting over the separation from the just man which was soon to happen; but it happened to him according to his wishes, since he was eager to depart from the world, that he might the sooner attain to the Lord whom he loved. Having, therefore, sailed into the harbour of the Romans when the foul spectacle was near its ending, the soldiers indeed were vexed at his slowness; but the bishop gladly obeyed them as they hurried him on.

VI.

From thence, therefore, they pushed on from the place called Portus (for the things that were happening to the holy martyr had already been noised abroad); we meet the brethren full of fear and joy, rejoicing, indeed, that we had been thought worthy of meeting Theophorus, but in fear, because he was being led to death. But certain of them he

exhorted to be quiet, since they were zealous, and
said they would appease the people, so that they
might not seek to destroy the just man; who
straightway knowing it in his spirit, and having
bade them all farewell, and having asked from
them for the true charity, and having discoursed
with them at greater length than he did in his
epistles, and having persuaded them not to grudge
him his hastening to the Lord; so with the bending
of the knees of all the brethren having implored
the Son of God on behalf of the churches, for the
cessation of the persecution, for the mutual love of
the brethren towards each other, he was led with
haste to the amphitheatre. Then having been
straightway cast in according to the original command of Cæsar, when the games were about to
come to an end (for there was then a notable feast
as they consider it, called in the Roman tongue
the thirteenth of the month, on which they eagerly
assembled), he was thus exposed to the wild beasts
beside the temple, so that by these means the
desire of the holy martyr Ignatius might be fulfilled—according to that which is written, the desire
of the just is acceptable—that he might not become
burdensome to any of the brethren by the collection of his remains, even as by anticipation in his
epistle he desired his own ending to happen.
For the harder parts alone of his remains were
left, which were conveyed to Antioch and de-
posited in linen, a pricelesss treasure left by the
grace which was in the martyr to the holy church.

VII.

Now these things happened on the thirteenth day before the calends of January, that is, on the twentieth of December, when Syra and Senecio were consuls of the Romans for the second time. Having been with tears eye-witnesses of these things, and having spent the whole night in the house, and having much implored the Lord with bended knees and prayers to make us weak men certain concerning the things that had just happened, after we had slept a little, some of us saw him suddenly standing by and embracing us; and some of us again saw the blessed Ignatius praying over us, and some of us saw him dripping with sweat, as though he had arrived after great toil and standing beside the Lord. Therefore with much joy, when we had seen these things and had compared the visions of the dreams, having celebrated the Lord, who is the giver of good things, and having deemed blessed the saint, we made manifest unto you both the day and the time, in order that, being gathered together at the time of the martyrdom, we might communicate with the athlete and noble martyr of Christ, who hath trampled under foot the devil, and hath finished in Jesus Christ our Lord the course of his desire, which was full of love towards Christ, to whom and with whom be the glory and the strength ascribed unto the Father together with the Holy Spirit for ever. Amen.

The Martyrdom of Polycarp.

Encyclic Epistle of the Church of Smyrna concerning the Martyrdom of S. Polycarp.

I.

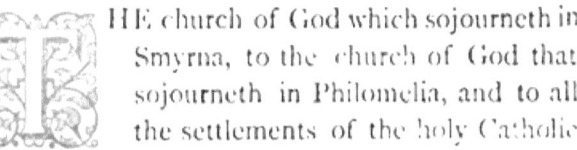HE church of God which sojourneth in Smyrna, to the church of God that sojourneth in Philomelia, and to all the settlements of the holy Catholic Church in every place, mercy, peace, and love from God the Father and our Lord Jesus Christ be multiplied unto you.

We have written unto you, brethren, the things respecting those who were martyred, and the blessed Polycarp, who made the persecution to cease, having as it were set his seal to it by his testimony. For almost all the things that went before happened in order that the Lord might show us from above the testimony that is according to the gospel; for he endured to be betrayed, even as did the Lord, that we might become imitators of him, not as considering the things that concern ourselves only, but also the things that concern our neighbours; for it belongeth to true and firm love not only to desire to be saved itself, but also that all the brethren should be saved.

II.

Blessed, therefore, and noble are all the testimonies that happened according to the will of God, for it is right that we should be the more careful, and should ascribe unto God the authority over all things. For who would not admire their nobility and endurance and obedience? who, though they were torn with stripes so that the internal arrangement of their flesh became evident even as far as the veins and arteries within, endured it, so that even the bystanders compassionated them and bemoaned them; and that others arrived at such a pitch of nobility that none of them would either sob or groan, showing all of us that in that hour the martyrs of Christ departed being tortured in the flesh, or rather that the Lord, standing by associated himself with them. And applying themselves to the grace of Christ, they despised the torture of this world, purchasing by the endurance of a single hour remission from eternal punishment; and the fire of their harsh tormentors was cold to them, for they had before their eyes to escape the eternal and never-quenched fire; and with the eyes of their heart they looked up to the good things that are reserved for those that endure, which neither hath ear heard, nor eye seen, nor hath it entered into the heart of man; but they have received glimpses of it who are no longer men but already angels. And in like manner they who had been condemned to the wild beasts endured dreadful punishments, lying upon beds of prickles, and punished with various other tortures, in order that, if it were possible, the tyrant might turn them from enduring faith to denial.

III.

For the devil contrived many things against them, but thanks be unto God, for he prevailed not against all. For the most noble Germanicus strengthened their cowardice through the patience that was in him, who also in a notable way fought against wild beasts. For when the proconsul would have persuaded him, saying that he had compassion upon his youth, he drew upon himself the wild beasts by force, wishing to be the sooner freed from this unjust and lawless life. From this, therefore, all the multitude, wondering at the nobleness of the God-loving and God-fearing race of Christians, called out, Away with the Atheists: let Polycarp be sought for.

IV.

But a certain man named Quintus, a Phrygian, who had newly come from Phrygia, when he saw the wild beasts, became afraid. This was he who constrained himself and others to come in of their own accord. This man, the proconsul, with much importunity, persuaded to swear and to sacrifice. On this account, brethren, we praise not them that give themselves up, since the gospel doth not so teach.

V.

But the most admirable Polycarp at the first, when he heard, was not disturbed, but desired to remain in the city. But the majority persuaded him to withdraw secretly; and he departed secretly to a villa not far from the city, and remained there with a few men, both night and day doing nothing but pray concerning all men, and for the churches that are in the world, as was his custom; and as he prayed he fell into a trance three days before he was taken; and he saw his pillow burning with fire, and he turned and said prophetically to those who were with him, I must be burned alive.

VI.

And when those who sought him continued in the pursuit, he departed unto another villa, and straightway the pursuers came upon him. And

when they found him not, they apprehended two
lads, of whom the one, when put to the torture,
confessed. For it was impossible for him to escape
their notice, since they who betrayed him were of
his own household. For the Eirenarchus, which is
the same office as Cleronomus, Herodes by name,
hasted to bring him into the arena, that he indeed
might fulfil his proper lot, by becoming a partaker
of Christ, and that they who betrayed him might
undergo the same punishment as Judas.

VII.

Having, therefore, with them the lad, on the day
of the preparation, at the hour of dinner, there came
out pursuers and horsemen, with their accustomed
arms, as though going out against a thief. And
having departed late at night, they found him lying
in a certain house, in an upper chamber. And he
might have departed from thence unto another place,
but was unwilling, saying, The will of the Lord be
done. And when he heard that they were present,
he descended and talked with them. And they who
were present wondered at the vigour of his age and
his soundness of body, and that they had had to
use so much trouble to capture so old a man. He
straightway commanded that meat and drink should
be set before them at that hour, as much as they
wished, and asked them to grant him an hour to
pray without molestation. And when they suffered
him, he stood and prayed, being full of the grace of

God, so that he could not be silent for two hours, and they that heard him were astonished, and many repented that they had come against so divine an old man.

VIII.

And when he had finished his prayer, having made mention of all who had at any time come into contact with him, both small and great, noble and ignoble, and of the whole Catholic Church throughout the world, when the hour of his departure had come, having seated him on an ass, they led him into the city, it being the great Sabbath. And the Tetrarch Herodes and his father Nicetes met him in a chariot, who, having transferred him into their car, seating themselves beside him, would have persuaded him, saying, What is the harm to say, Cæsar. Cæsar, and to sacrifice, and to do such like things, and to be saved? But he at the first did not answer them; but when they persisted, he said, I will not do that which ye advise me. But they, when they had failed to persuade him, said unto him dreadful words, and thrust him with such haste from the chariot that in descending from the car he grazed his shin. And paying no attention to it, as though he had suffered nothing, he proceeded zealously, with eagerness being led to the arena, there being such a noise in the arena that no one could even be heard.

IX.

But to Polycarp, as he entered the arena, there came a voice from Heaven, saying, Be strong, and play the man, O Polycarp. And the speaker no man saw; but the voice those of our people who were present heard. And when he was brought in there was a great tumult, when men heard that Polycarp was apprehended. Then, when he had been brought in, the proconsul asked him if he was Polycarp. And when he confessed, he would have persuaded him to deny, saying, Have respect unto thine age, and other things like these, as is their custom to say: Swear by the fortunes of Cæsar; Repent; Say, Away with the Atheists. But Polycarp, when he had looked with a grave face at all the multitude of lawless heathen in the arena, having beckoned unto them with his hand, sighed, and looking up unto heaven, said, Away with the Atheists! And when the proconsul pressed him, and said, Swear, and I will release thee, revile Christ; Polycarp said, Eighty and six years have I served him, and in nothing hath he wronged me; and how, then, can I blaspheme my King, who saved me?

X.

But when he again persisted, and said, Swear by the fortune of Cæsar, he answered, If thou art vainly confident that I shall swear by the fortune

of Cæsar, as thou suggestest, and pretendest to be
ignorant of me who I am, hear distinctly, I am a
Christian. But if thou desirest to learn the scheme
of Christianity, give me a day to speak, and hearken
unto me. The proconsul said, Persuade the people.
Polycarp said, I have thought thee indeed worthy
to receive explanation, for we have been taught to
render such honour as is fitting, and as does not
injure us, to the powers and authorities ordained
of God; but those I consider not worthy that I
should make my defence before them.

XI.

But the proconsul said unto him, I have wild
beasts; I will deliver thee unto them, unless thou
repentest. But he said, Call them, for repentance
from the better to the worse is impossible for us;
but it is a good thing to change from evil deeds
to just ones. But he said again unto him, I will
cause thee to be consumed by fire if thou despisest
the wild beasts, unless thou repentest. But Polycarp said, Thou threatenest me with fire that
burneth but for a season, and is soon quenched.
For thou art ignorant of the fire of the judgment
to come, and of the eternal punishment reserved
for the wicked. But why delayest thou? Bring
whatever thou wishest.

XII.

While he was saying these and more things, he was filled with courage and joy, and his face was filled with grace ; so that he not only was not troubled and confused by the things said unto him, but, on the contrary, the proconsul was astonished, and sent his herald into the midst of the arena to proclaim a third time : Polycarp has confessed himself to be a Christian. When this had been said by the herald, the whole multitude, both of Gentiles and Jews, that inhabit Smyrna, with irrestrainable anger and a loud voice, called out, This is the teacher of impiety, the father of the Christians, the destroyer of your gods, who teacheth many neither to sacrifice nor to worship the gods. Saying these things, they shouted out, and asked the Asiarch Philip to let loose the lion at Polycarp. But Philip replied that it was not lawful for him to do so, since he had finished his exhibition of wild beasts. Then it seemed good unto them to shout with one voice that Polycarp should be burnt alive ; for it was necessary that the vision that appeared unto him on his pillow should be fulfilled, when, seeing it burning, he prayed, and said prophetically, turning to the faithful who were with him, I must be burnt alive.

XIII.

These things, therefore, happened with greater speed than can be narrated, the multitude quickly collecting logs and brushwood from the workshops and baths, the Jews especially lending their services zealously for this purpose, as is their custom. But when the pyre was ready, having put off all his garments, and having loosed his girdle, he essayed to take off his shoes; not being in the habit of doing this previously, because each of the faithful used to strive which should be the first to touch his body, for, on account of his good conversation, he was, even before his martyrdom, adorned with every good gift. Straightway, therefore, they put around him the implements prepared for the pyre. And when they were about to nail him to it, he said, Suffer me thus, for he who gave me to abide the fire will also allow me, without the security of your nails, to remain on the pyre without moving.

XIV.

They, therefore, did not nail him, but bound him. But he, having placed his hands behind him, and being bound like a notable ram appointed for offering out of a great flock, prepared as a whole burnt-offering acceptable unto God, having looked up unto heaven, said, O Lord God Almighty, Father of thy beloved and blessed Son Jesus Christ, through whom we have received our knowledge concerning thee, the God of angels and powers, and of the whole creation, and of all the race of the just who live before thee, I thank thee that thou hast deemed me worthy of this day and hour, that I should have my portion in the number of thy martyrs, in the cup of thy Christ, unto the resurrection of eternal life, both of the soul and body, in the incorruptibility of the Holy Spirit. By means of which may I be received before thee this day as a rich and acceptable sacrifice, even as thou hast prepared and made manifest beforehand, and hast fulfilled, thou who art the unerring and true God. On this account, above all things I praise thee, I bless thee, I glorify thee, together with the eternal and heavenly Jesus Christ thy beloved Son, with whom to thee and the Holy Spirit be glory both now and for ever. Amen.

XV.

And when he had uttered the Amen, and had finished his prayer, the men over the fire kindled it. And a great flame breaking out, we, to whom it was given to see, saw a great wonder; for this also were we preserved that we might announce what happened to the rest of mankind. For the fire, assuming the form of a vault, like the sail of a vessel filled with the wind, defended the body of the martyr round about; and it was in the midst of the flame not like flesh burning, but like bread baking, or like gold and silver glowing in a furnace. And we perceived such a sweet-smelling savour, as though from the breath of incense or some other precious perfume.

XVI.

At last these wicked men, perceiving that his body could not be consumed by the fire, commanded the slaughterer to come near and plunge in a sword. And when they had done this, there came out a dove and an abundance of blood, so that it quenched the fire, and all the multitude wondered that there was such a difference between the unbelievers and the elect. Of whom this most admirable martyr Polycarp was one, having been in our time the apostolic and prophetic teacher and bishop of the Catholic church which is in Smyrna. For every word which he uttered from his mouth both hath been fulfilled and shall be fulfilled.

XVII.

But the evil one, who is the opponent and envier and enemy to the race of men, beholding both the greatness of his testimony and his blameless conversation from the beginning, how he was crowned with the crown of immortality, and how he carried off a prize that could not be spoken against, contrived that not even a relic of him should be taken by us, though many desired to do this, and to communicate with his holy flesh. He suborned, therefore, Nicetes, the father of Herodes, and the brother of Alce, to make interest with the governor so as not to give his body to the tomb, Lest, said he, they abandon the crucified and begin to worship this man. And these things they said at the suggestion and instance of the Jews, who also kept watch when we were about to take the body from the fire, not knowing that we shall never be able to abandon Christ, who suffered for the salvation of the whole world of those who are saved, the blameless on the behalf of the sinner, nor to worship any one else. Him we adore as the Son of God; but the martyrs, as the disciples and imitators of the Lord, we love according to their deserts, on account of their incomparable love for their King and Master, with whom may it be our lot to be partners and fellow disciples.

XVIII.

Therefore, the centurion, seeing the strife that had risen among the Jews, placed the body in the midst of the fire and burned it. Thus we, having afterwards taken up his bones, more valuable than precious stones, laid them where it was suitable. There in accordance with our powers, when we are gathered together in exultation and joy, the Lord will enable us to celebrate the birthday of the martyrs, both for the memory of those who have contended, and for the exercise and preparation of those to come.

XIX.

Such were the things that happened to the blessed Polycarp, who together with those from Philadelphia was the twelfth who suffered martyrdom in Smyrna; but he alone is held in memory by all, so that he is spoken of in every place even by the gentiles; not only being a distinguished teacher, but also an eminent martyr, whose testimony we desire to imitate, since it happened according to the gospel of Christ. For having overcome by patience the unjust governor, and so having received the crown of immortality, rejoicing together with the apostles and all the just, he glorifieth God and the Father, and blesseth our Lord Jesus Christ the Saviour of our souls, and the pilot of our bodies, and the shepherd of the Catholic Church throughout the world.

XX.

Ye therefore desired that the things that had happened should be shown unto you more at length; but we for the present have related them unto you briefly by means of our brother Mark. Now do ye, when ye have read these things, send them unto the brethren farther off, that they also may glorify the Lord, who is making a selection from among his own servants. To him who is able to bring us all in, by his grace and gift, into his eternal kingdom, through his only-begotten Son Jesus Christ; to him be the glory, honour, strength, majesty for ever. Salute all the saints. They who are with us salute you, and Evarestus who wrote these things, and all his house.

XXI.

Now the blessed Polycarp was martyred on the second day of the month Xanthicus, on the twenty-fifth of April, on the great Sabbath, at the eighth hour. But he was apprehended by Herodes, when Philip of Tralles was high priest, Statius Quadratus being proconsul, and Jesus Christ king for ever, to whom be glory, honour, majesty, and eternal throne, from generation to generation. Amen.

XXII.

We pray, brethren, that you may fare well, walking by the word of the gospel of Jesus Christ, with whom be glory to God and the Father, and the Holy Spirit, for the salvation of the holy elect, even as the blessed Polycarp hath borne witness, in whose steps may we be found in the kingdom of Jesus Christ. These things have been transcribed by Gaius, from the manuscript of Irenæus the disciple of Polycarp, who also was a fellow citizen to Irenæus. But I, Socrates, made a copy in Corinth from the manuscript of Gaius. Grace be with you all.

But I, Pionius, afterwards copied them from the above written, having sought them out after that the blessed Polycarp had made them manifest to me by a revelation, as I will show in what follows; having gathered them together, when they had already become almost obliterated by time, in order that the Lord Jesus Christ may gather me also together with his elect, unto his heavenly kingdom, to whom be glory with the Father, and the Holy Spirit, world without end. Amen.

The Syriac Version of the Epistles of S. Ignatius.

The Epistle of S. Ignatius the Bishop to Polycarp.[1]

IGNATIUS, who is Theophorus, to Polycarp Bishop of Smyrna, who himself rather is visited by God the Father and by Jesus Christ our Lord, much peace.

Forasmuch as thy mind, which is confirmed in God as upon a rock immovable, is acceptable to me, I praise God the more abundantly for having been accounted worthy of thy countenance, which I long for in God. I beseech thee, therefore, by the grace with which thou art clothed, to add to thy course, and pray for all men that they may be saved, and require things becoming with all diligence of flesh and of spirit. Be careful for unanimity, than which nothing is more excellent. Bear all men as our Lord beareth thee. Be patient with all men in love, as [indeed] thou art. Be constant in prayer. Ask more understanding

---

[1] The translation here given is extracted from the "Corpus Ignatianum" of Dr. Cureton. Cf. Introduction x. xliv.

than what thou [already] hast. Be watchful, for thou possessest a spirit that sleepeth not. Speak with all men according to the will of God. Bear the infirmities of all men like a perfect combatant; for where the labour is much, much also is the gain. If thou love the good disciples only, thou hast no grace : rather subdue those who are evil by gentleness. All wounds are not healed by one medicine. Allay cutting by tenderness. Be wise as the serpent in every thing, and innocent as the dove as to those things which are requisite. On this account art thou [both] of flesh and of spirit, that thou mayest allure those things which are seen before thy face, and ask respecting those things which are hidden from thee, that they may be revealed to thee, that thou mayest be lacking in nothing, and mayest abound in all gifts. The time requireth, as a pilot a ship, and as he who standeth in the tempest the haven, that thou shouldest be worthy of God. Be vigilant as a combatant of God. That which is promised to us is life eternal, incorruptible, of which things thou also art persuaded. In every thing I will be instead of thy soul, and my bonds which thou hast loved. Let not those who seem to be something and teach strange doctrines astound thee, but stand in the truth, like a combatant who is smitten : for it is [the part] of a great combatant that he should be smitten and conquer. More especially on God's account it behoveth us to endure every thing, that He also may endure us. Be diligent

[even] more than thou art. Be discerning of the times. Expect Him who is above the times, Him to whom there are no times, Him who is unseen, Him who for our sakes was seen, Him who is impalpable, Him who is impassible, Him who for our sakes suffered, Him who endured every thing in every form for our sakes.

Let not the widows be neglected: on our Lord's account be thou their guardian, and let nothing be done without thy will; neither do thou any thing without the will of God; nor indeed doest thou. Stand well. Let there be frequent assemblies. Ask every man by his name. Despise not slaves and handmaids; but neither let them be contemptuous; but let them serve the more, as for the glory of God, that they may be accounted worthy of a better freedom which is of God. Let them not desire to be set free from the common [property], that they may not be found the slaves of lusts. Fly from evil arts; but rather discourse respecting them. Tell my sisters that they love in the Lord, and that their husbands be sufficient for them in flesh and in spirit. Then again, charge my brethren, in the name of our Lord Jesus Christ, that they love their wives as our Lord his church. If any one be able in strength to continue in chastity to the honour of the flesh of our Lord, let him continue without boasting; if he boasts he is lost: if he become known apart from the Bishop he has corrupted himself. It is becoming, therefore, to men and women who marry, that they marry by the council of the Bishop, that the marriage may be in our Lord, and not in lust. Let every thing, therefore, be for the honour of God.

Look to the Bishop, that God also may look upon you. I will be instead of the souls of those who are subject to the Bishop, and the Presbyters, and the Deacons; with them may I have a portion near God. Labour together with one another; make the struggle together, run together, suffer together, sleep together, rise together. As stewards of God, and his domestics and ministers, please him and serve him, that ye may receive the wages from him. Let none of you rebel. Let your baptism be to you as armour, and faith as a helmet, and love as a spear, and patience as a panoply. Let your treasures be your good works, that ye may receive the gift of God, as it is just. Let your spirit be enduring towards each other in meekness, as God towards you. I rejoice in you at all times. The Christian has not power over himself, but is ready to be subject to God. I salute him who is accounted worthy to go to Antioch in my stead, as I charged thee.

His Second Epistle, to the Ephesians.

IGNATIUS, who is Theophorus, to the Church which is blessed in the greatness of God the Father, and perfected; to her who was separated from eternity to be at all times for glory that abideth and changeth not, and is perfected and chosen in the purpose of truth, by the will of the Father of Jesus Christ our God; to her who is worthy of happiness; to her who is at Ephesus in Jesus Christ in joy unblameable; much peace.

Forasmuch as your well beloved name is acceptable to me in God, which ye have acquired by nature by a right and just will, and also by faith and love of Jesus Christ our Saviour, and ye are imitators of God, and fervent in the blood of God, and have speedily accomplished a work congenial to you; for when ye heard that I was bound from actions for the sake of the common name and hope—and I hope through your prayers to be devoured of beasts at Rome, that by means of this of which I am accounted worthy I may be em-

powered with strength to be a disciple of God—
ye were diligent to come and see me. Forasmuch, therefore, as we have received your abundance in the name of God by Onesimus, who is
your Bishop in love unutterable, whom I pray that
ye love in Jesus Christ our Lord, and that all of
you be like him; for blessed is He who hath given
you such a Bishop, as ye deserve; but forasmuch as love suffereth me not to be silent respecting you, on this account I have been forward
to entreat you to be diligent in the will of God;
for so long as no one lust is implanted in you
which is able to torment you, lo, ye live in God.
I rejoice in you, and offer supplication on account
of you, Ephesians, a church renowned in all ages.
For those who are carnal are not able to do
spiritual things, neither the spiritual carnal things;
likewise neither faith those things which are foreign
to faith, nor lack of faith what is faith's. For those
things which ye have done in the flesh even they
are spiritual, because ye have done every thing in
Jesus Christ, and ye are prepared for the building
of God the Father, and are raised up on high by
the engine of Jesus Christ, which is the Cross, and
ye are drawn by the rope, which is the Holy
Ghost; and your pulley is your faith, and
your love is the way that leadeth up on high to
God. Pray for all men, for there is hope of repentance for them, that they may be accounted worthy
of God. By your works rather let them be instructed. Against their harsh words be ye con-

ciliatory in meekness of mind and gentleness: against their blasphemies do ye pray: and against their error be ye armed with faith: and against their fierceness be ye peaceful and quiet: and be ye not astounded by them. Let us then be imitators of our Lord in meekness, and [emulous] as to who shall be injured, and oppressed, and defrauded more [than the rest]. The work is not of promise, unless a man be found in the power of faith even to the end. It is better that a man be silent when he is something than that he should be speaking when he is not: that by those things which he speaks he should act, and by those things of which he is silent he should be known. My spirit boweth down to the Cross, which is an offence to those who do not believe, but to you salvation and life eternal. There was concealed from the ruler of this world the virginity of Mary, and the birth of our Lord, and the three mysteries of the shout, which were done in the quietness of God from the star. And here at the manifestation of the Son magic began to be destroyed, and all bonds were loosed, and the ancient kingdom and the error of evil was destroyed. From hence all things were moved together, and the destruction of death was devised, and there was the commencement of that which is perfected in God.

The Third Epistle of the same S. Ignatius.

IGNATIUS, who is Theophorus, to the Church which has been pitied in the greatness of the Father Most High; to her who presideth in the place of the country of the Romans, who is worthy of God, and worthy of life and happiness and praise and remembrance, and is worthy of prosperity, and presideth in love, and is perfected in the law of Christ blameless, much peace.

Long since have I prayed to God that I might be accounted worthy to behold your faces, which are worthy of God: now therefore being bound in Jesus Christ, I hope to meet you and salute you if there be the will that I should be accounted worthy to the end. For the beginning is well disposed, if I be accounted worthy to attain to the end, that I may receive my portion without hindrance through suffering. For I am afraid of your love, lest it should injure me. For you, indeed, it is easy for you to do what you wish; but for me, it is difficult for me to be accounted worthy of God, if indeed you spare me not. For there is no other time like this, that I should be accounted worthy of God; neither will ye, if ye be silent, be found in a better work than this. If ye leave me I shall be the word of God; but if ye love my flesh, again am I to myself a voice. Ye will not give me any thing better than this, that I should be sacrificed to God while the altar is ready; that ye may be in one concord in love, and may praise God the Father through Jesus Christ our Lord, because he has accounted a Bishop worthy to be God's, having called him from the East to the West. It is good that I should set from the world in God, that I may rise in Him in life.

Ye have never envied any one. Ye have taught others. Pray only for strength to be given to me from within and from without, that I may not only speak, but also may be willing; and not that I may be called a Christian only, but also that I may be found to be [one]: for if I am found to be [one], I am also able to be called [so]. Then [indeed] shall I be faithful, when I am no longer seen in the world. For there is nothing which is seen that is good. The work is not [a matter] of persuasion, but Christianity is great when the world hateth it. I write to all the Churches, and declare to all men that I die willingly for God, if it be that ye hinder me not. I entreat you, be not [affected] towards me by love that is unseasonable. Leave me to be the beasts', that through them I may be accounted worthy of God. I am the wheat of God, and by the teeth of the beasts I am ground, that I may be found the pure bread of God. With provoking provoke ye the beasts, that they may be a grave for me, and may leave nothing of my body, that even after I am fallen asleep I may not be a burden upon any one. Then shall I be in truth a disciple of Jesus Christ, when the world seeth not even my body. Intreat our Lord for me, that through these instruments I may be found a sacrifice to God.

I do not charge you like Peter and Paul, who are Apostles, but I am one condemned: they indeed are free, but I am a slave even until now. But if I suffer, I shall be the freedman of Jesus Christ, and I shall rise from the dead in Him free. And now, being bound, I learn to desire nothing. From Syria and even to Rome I am cast among beasts, by sea and by land, by night and by day, being bound between ten leopards, which are the band of soldiers, who, even while I do good to them, do evil the more to me. But I am the rather instructed by their injury, but not on this account am I justified to myself. I rejoice in the beasts that are prepared for me, and I pray that they may be quickly found for me; and I will provoke them to devour me speedily: and not as that which is afraid of some other men, and does not approach them even should they not be willing to approach me, I will go with violence against them. Know me from myself. What is expedient for

me? Let nothing envy me of those that are seen
and that are not seen, that I should be accounted
worthy of Jesus Christ. Fire and the cross, and
the beasts that are prepared, amputation of the
limbs, and scattering of the bones, and crushing of
the whole body, hard torments of the devil, let
these come upon me, and only may I be accounted
worthy of Jesus Christ. The pains of the birth
stand over me, and my love is crucified, and
there is no fire in me for another love. I do
not desire the food of corruption, neither the
desires of this world. The bread of God I seek,
which is the flesh of Jesus Christ, and his blood I
seek, a drink which is love incorruptible. My
spirit saluteth you, and the love of the Churches
which received me as the name of Jesus Christ, for
even those who were near to the way in the flesh
preceded me in every city. Now, therefore, being
about to arrive shortly at Rome, I know many
things in God; but I moderate myself, that I may
not perish through boasting; for now it behoveth
me to fear the more, and not to regard those who
puff me up. For they who say to me such things,
scourge me: for I love to suffer, but I do not
know if I am worthy. For to many zeal is not
seen; but with me it has war: I have need therefore of meekness, by which the ruler of this world
is destroyed. I am able to write to you of
heavenly things; but I fear lest I should do you
an injury. Know me from myself. For I am
cautious, lest ye should not be able to receive it

and should be perplexed. For even I, not because I am bound, and am able to know heavenly things; and the places of angels, and the station of the powers that are seen and that are not seen, on this account am I a disciple : for I am far short of the perfection which is worthy of God. Be ye perfectly safe in the patience of Jesus Christ our God.

www.ingramcontent.com/pod-product-compliance
Lightning Source LLC
Chambersburg PA
CBHW032150230426
43672CB00011B/2508